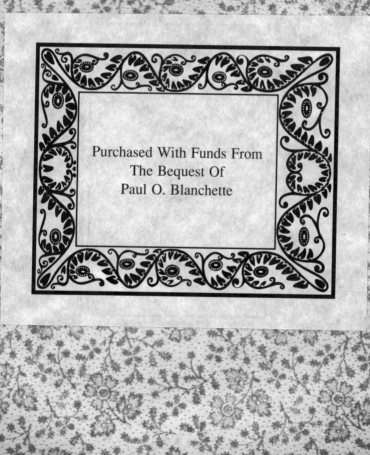

FROM MY HEART TO YOURS: Life Lessons on Faith, Family, and Friendship
Copyright © 2007 Robin McGraw

Published in Nashville, Tennessee, by Thomas Nelson, Inc.

Project Editor: Jessica Inman
Art Direction and Design: Linda Bourdeaux, lindamaybe@thedesigndesk.com

ISBN-10: 1–4041–0521–2
ISBN-13: 978–1–4041–0521–8

Printed and bound in the United States of America

www.thomasnelson.com

ROBIN MCGRAW

FROM MY HEART TO YOURS

Life Lessons on Faith, Family, & Friendship

THOMAS NELSON
Since 1798

NASHVILLE   DALLAS   MEXICO CITY   RIO DE JANEIRO   BEIJING

Contents

1

FAITH

NO MATTER HOW ORGANIZED AND
VIGILANT WE ARE, LIFE STILL HAS A WAY
OF BRINGING US TO OUR KNEES.

CHOOSE TO BE WHO YOU'RE MEANT TO BE

WHEN SOMETHING INSIDE JUST WON'T GIVE UP

CHOOSING AN ATTITUDE OF GRATITUDE

GIVING YOUR CHILDREN UP TO GOD

ACTING ON YOUR GOD-GIVEN GIFTS AND DESIRES

EMBRACING THE WOMAN GOD CREATED

THERE'S A REASON FOR EVERYTHING

WORKING WITH PASSION AND PURPOSE

SPEAKING YOUR MIND—AND HEART

WE MAKE OUR DECISIONS, AND THEN OUR DECISIONS TURN AROUND AND MAKE US.

— *Francis Boreham*

CHOOSE TO BE
Who You're Meant to Be

I believe that in order for a woman to experience true happiness, fulfillment, and peace, she needs to know two things: who she is, and who she is meant to be. They're not the same thing: the first one has to do with the reality of your life, and the second one has to do with your purpose for being in this world, which is something each of us has to discover for ourselves and cannot be dictated by any other person in our lives—not by our husband, parents, children, employers, or friends.

I believe it's gotten harder and harder to tell the difference between who we are and who we're meant to be. So much of the time, we lose ourselves just trying to keep up with the frantic pace of life. We drag ourselves out of bed in the morning, already half an hour behind, and spend much of the day responding to the needs and demands of others. Somewhere along the line, we often lose track of the essential feminine self—that unique, life-giving entity that invigorates our beings and warms the souls of the people we love.

But we don't have to lose that feminine self, and the way to hold on to her is to accept nothing less than being simply the best—the best we can be in the roles we choose for ourselves: wife, mother, daughter, sister, and friend.

I also believe we were put on this earth to enjoy lives of joy and abundance, and that is what I want for you and for me. I hope you're excited about whatever phase of life you're in: excited about being a woman in this day and time, excited about being the woman God created you to be. It's all there for the choosing, because, in the core of my soul, I believe that how you live, how I live, how we all live as women is largely a matter of choice. We have the power to choose joy in strenuous circumstances. We have the ability to choose a good attitude when everyone around us is grumpy. We have the privilege to choose the words we speak and how we speak them, or to simply remain quiet.

I BELIEVE THAT HOW YOU LIVE, HOW I LIVE, HOW WE ALL LIVE AS WOMEN IS LARGELY A MATTER OF CHOICE.

I imagine that a lot of women who hear me say this may think, *That's easy for you to say. You can choose whatever you want because you live in a wonderful house with a successful man who loves you, and you can probably have anything you want—you're a privileged person.* And all that is true. But do you know what the real privilege is? The real privilege is being free to embrace the joyful aspects of life and reject the hurtful ones—to choose to do what's working, and to turn your back on what isn't. It's a privilege to have the right to take charge of your existence and be excited about your life.

Too often, people think they need a lot of costly stuff to be happy. The first apartment Phil and I moved into was a whopping 420 square feet of linoleum and worn nylon pile, and I used to drive a 1962 Comet with bright turquoise paint that looked as if it had been brushed on. When I was a kid, the only spoons I had in my mouth were stainless steel, not silver. Still, I always felt fortunate to be who I was, and excited by the prospect of what life held for me.

We are defined not by the station in life into which we are born, nor by our pedigree, race or religion, but by the choices we make. And it is through the integrity of our choices that we create the life we long for. Embrace the privilege to choose how you will live rather than taking life as it comes along—not so you'll make the same choices I made, but so you will make the choices that are right for you.

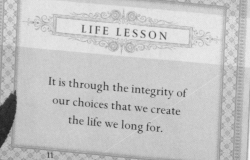

LIFE LESSON

It is through the integrity of our choices that we create the life we long for.

GOOD INSTINCTS USUALLY TELL YOU WHAT TO DO
LONG BEFORE YOUR HEAD HAS FIGURED IT OUT.

— *Michael Burke*

WHEN SOMETHING INSIDE

Just Won't Give Up

It's not always easy to stick up for yourself. People in authority can be intimidating, especially when they're not accustomed to being challenged. And there's always a chance that you'll raise a ruckus, only to find out you were wrong and end up looking like an idiot. But I'd rather risk looking like an idiot than feel like one for being too intimidated to stand up for me and mine.

I was in just such a situation a few years ago with my son Jordan. He was in seventh grade and playing a lot of sports when he came in one night and showed me a little knot-like bruise on his shin. He wasn't sure when he got it and it didn't hurt, so we figured he got it playing football and, since the season had just ended, we decided to wait for it to go away on its own. Then basketball season started and Jordan began practicing after school and competing on weekends. He soon began complaining of pain in his lower back, which struck me as odd for a twelve-year-old kid. I began to wonder if maybe he'd hurt his back during football season and, remembering how Phillip had wrecked his body playing college ball, decided to take Jordan to the orthopedist to make sure everything was all right.

So I took Jordan in and the doctor examined him and said that it's common for active kids his age to experience growing pains—yes, that's what they call them—and when their backs hurt it's because as the vertebrae grow, tiny amounts of gaseous material can get between them and cause discomfort. The doctor offered to do an X-ray just to make sure there was nothing wrong. I said that sounded good, and then had another thought.

"Doctor," I said, "while you're x-raying Jordan's back, would you also please do this bump on his leg?"

"What bump are you talking about?" he said.

"It's not very big," I said, "and it's right here on his shin bone. He's had it for a while now, since the end of football season."

The doctor looked at it impassively. "It doesn't look like anything to me. I'm sure it's just from getting hit a few times."

That's the moment, the intimidating moment when an expert tells you the truth about a situation and you're expected to accept it, thank him, and go away. Except the expert's truth contradicts something deep in your gut, and you know his truth is different from your truth; and you've got to choose between being a good girl who bows to authority and being a no-nonsense woman who's not afraid to look like a fool when she's acting in the service of those she loves.

I took a breath and spoke. "Yes, but it's been there for at least three weeks now, and if it were a bruise it would be gone by now."

———————— ✦ ————————

YOU HAVE TO CHOOSE BETWEEN BEING A GOOD GIRL WHO BOWS TO AUTHORITY AND BEING A NO-NONSENSE WOMAN WHO'S NOT AFRAID TO LOOK LIKE A FOOL WHEN SHE'S ACTING IN THE SERVICE OF THOSE SHE LOVES.

"Maybe yes and maybe no. Some bruises take longer to heal than others, and we don't like to x-ray every little bump that shows up on these kids. You don't want to expose a young boy to too many X-rays, you know."

"Yes, I know," I said. "But I also know that every other bruise this child has had has healed in less than a week and it worries me that this one is taking so long to disappear. So would you please x-ray it, just to be safe? Please?" He looked at me with exasperation but agreed to do it.

I was waiting in the examining room when the doctor reappeared with a serious look on his face. "How long exactly has he had this knot on his leg?" he said.

"He noticed it about three weeks ago but it may have been there longer," I said.

"I am glad I did that X-ray. We have some cause for concern here, so I'm scheduling an MRI upstairs. They're waiting on him, so why don't you take him up?"

As it turned out, Jordan's bump was important but not serious. He had a benign mass growing on his tibia and the orthopedist—who was also a surgeon—was able to remove it. Jordan spent a couple of nights in the hospital; the mass never returned.

What returns for me, however, is the memory of that afternoon, and how a child's well-being was so utterly dependent on his mother's persistence rather than a physician's expertise. It left an indelible imprint on me, and confirmed something I'd learned long ago: you don't have to have a medical degree to know when something is wrong with your kid, and you don't have to apologize to a nurse or a doctor or anyone else for saying so.

It's very important that women not be afraid to stand up for themselves. Too many women are willing to abdicate their responsibility as mature, thinking adults because they have been taught that they should defer to authority, especially when the authority is a man. We women can be a little too quick to abandon our inner wisdom when someone in a position of power contradicts it.

I am not afraid to question authority. I am not willing to give my power away to anybody just because he wears a white coat. I believe I am accountable for whatever happens to me and to those under my care, and that this is true for all of us. I believe it is my responsibility to stand up for what I believe is right, no matter how uncomfortable it feels. Moreover, I believe that is what God wants me to do. He blessed me with the intelligence to think for myself and with parents who taught me to trust my judgment, and I believe I would be squandering these gifts from above if I did not put them to good use here on earth.

LIFE LESSON

We have a responsibility to stand up for what we believe is right, no matter how uncomfortable it feels.

NO DUTY IS MORE URGENT THAN
THAT OF RETURNING THANKS.

— *Saint Ambrose*

CHOOSING AN ATTITUDE
of Gratitude

Alot of people have a great life, but they just don't see it. They choose to focus not on what they actually have but on what they believe they lack, and they miss what life is all about. Some people never have enough; no matter how devoted their mate is, they always wish he (or she) were fitter, richer, or more attractive. No matter how accomplished their kids are, they always think they could have won a bigger trophy or higher academic honor if only they'd tried a little harder. No matter how nice their car or how gracious their home, they always want a bigger or a fancier model. And while I firmly believe in striving for a good life, I also believe you have to recognize when you have it good, and thank God for what you have.

I have a good life. I wake up every morning in my wonderful home and thank God for all the joy and abundance with which He has blessed me. But, while I love this house, it is not what makes me wake up happy every day. If Phillip and I were not solid in our commitment to each other, this house wouldn't do us a lick of good; it would just be a bigger space in which to be lonely.

I WAKE UP EVERY MORNING AND THANK GOD FOR ALL THE JOY AND ABUNDANCE WITH WHICH HE HAS BLESSED ME.

It doesn't matter where we live; we started out in a one-bedroom apartment, and I could go back there today. I swear to you I could leave this 90210 lifestyle, throw on some cut-off jeans and a T-shirt, and go back to that little apartment in Denton, Texas, with my husband. We'd be just as happy as we could be, as long as we were together and proud of each other and doing what was important.

Yes, I love the mosaic floors and crystal chandeliers in this house, but not any more than a certain pair of wooden barstools that graced our apartment when Phillip was in grad school. I'll never forget this. He was off working with his father for the weekend and I decided I was going to do something fun with the apartment and surprise him when he got back. I had eight dollars left over from that week's budget to play around with, so I went to the supermarket and bought a can of tangerine orange paint and a brush for five dollars, and a little ivy plant with the three dollars I had left. I came home to our bland little apartment with the beige walls and brown carpet and painted these two bar stools a bright tangerine color and set them next to the breakfast bar where they glowed like a Tahitian sunset. I took the green ivy and set it on the bar so it cascaded off the edge onto the seat of that shimmering barstool, and I thought it was the most beautiful thing I had ever seen. And in many ways, it still is. Its preciousness transcended the eight dollars it cost me to create it, because it was born in my heart and made real by my hands. I imagined it and made it happen. To me, there's nothing better.

LIFE LESSON

As important as it is to strive for a good life, it's also important to recognize when we have it good, and give thanks to God.

I HAVE HELD MANY THINGS IN MY HANDS, AND
I HAVE LOST THEM ALL; BUT WHATEVER I HAVE
PLACED IN GOD'S HANDS, THAT I STILL POSSESS.

— *Corrie Ten Boom*

up to God

Something was wrong with Jay. Every time I fed him, he vomited so forcefully that it shot across the room. I knew projectile vomiting was common in infants but this was happening every time he ate. We'd seen the pediatrician five days earlier and he'd sent me away with some tranquilizer drops and told me to relax, but Jay still wasn't eating and he was starting to look listless and weak. I called and insisted that the doctor see the baby again.

There was a gravelly sigh at the other end of the line but he agreed to see Jay in the morning. I put the baby to bed that night thinking, *Relax, Robin—you'll take him in tomorrow. Everything will be fine, you'll see.*

I woke up feeling unusually well rested and then realized why: the baby hadn't woken me up in the middle of the night to feed him. I felt great for a nanosecond until my rational mind kicked in and I thought, *No, that's not right—it's too soon for him to sleep through the night, he gets too hungry; it just can't be.* I ran down the hall to the nursery.

Jay was lying motionless in his crib except for his poor little belly going up and down as he breathed. He was so weak, he couldn't cry loudly enough to wake me to feed him. He looked as if he were starving to death, which wasn't far from the truth. It was only 8:15 and the doctor's office wouldn't open for another forty-five minutes, but I wasn't about to stand around doing nothing. Phillip had already left for work, so I threw on some clothes, scooped Jay out of his crib, then called my sister-in-law Donna and asked if she could come over right away and take me to the pediatrician. I wanted to devote all my attention to Jay and not worry about driving; besides, Donna had three kids of her own and was no stranger to medical emergencies.

I'D RATHER RISK LOOKING LIKE AN IDIOT THAN FEEL LIKE ONE FOR BEING TOO INTIMIDATED TO STAND UP FOR ME AND MINE.

We arrived at the doctor's office before he did and I remember pacing in circles around the reception area thinking, *Hurry, please hurry . . . I can't wait, I can't wait.* Then he walked in and I went right up to him with Jay in my arms and said, "There is something wrong with this baby and I'm tired of you telling me it's because I'm a nervous mother. You need to see him right now." He told me to bring him on back into the examining room.

I laid Jay on the table and unwrapped his blanket. The doctor walked over, looked at the baby, and then looked at me. "How long has this been going on?" As if he didn't know. "What do you mean? I had him here five days ago and you told me I was a nervous mother and sent me home with tranquilizing drops. I've been calling you all week and you keep telling me to wait another day and I've been trying to tell you that there's something wrong with him." He took another look at Jay and called over his shoulder to the nurse to alert the hospital that we were on our way.

"We have to get him into surgery right away," he said. "I'll explain when we get there." He then headed out to his car and we headed out to ours.

Donna drove straight to the hospital; Phillip met us there. When the pediatrician arrived he said he believed that Jay had a condition known as pyloric stenosis, a digestive disorder affecting three out of a thousand babies born in the United States. What happens is the muscles in the lower part of the baby's stomach, known as the pylorus, thicken and enlarge, making it impossible for food to empty out of the stomach into the small intestine. As food builds up in the stomach, the baby vomits explosively, expelling everything it takes in and eventually growing malnourished and weak because its body isn't receiving any nutrients.

The doctor reassured us that he could perform a single operation to open the passage between Jay's stomach and his intestines and, after a couple of days in the hospital for observation, he could go home and would be just fine.

They began prepping Jay for surgery. They were having trouble inserting an intravenous line because he was dehydrated and his little veins had collapsed, so they started looking for a spot on his scalp. Phillip knew I would not be able to bear seeing a needle in his poor little head, so he suggested they try to put it in his hand. They balled his hand into a tiny fist, found a vein, and tried to insert the needle but it wouldn't go.

They tried again but they still couldn't get it in. I was holding him and he was screaming, but he was so weak that all that came out were squeaky gasping sounds. They said they would try the hand one more time before inserting the needle in his scalp. This time, by the grace of God, they managed to insert the IV.

My poor baby was so weak, he didn't have the energy to cry. He lay in my arms, sobbing and trembling, and I remember thinking, *Of all the things that have happened in my life, this is the worst, the absolute worst.*

Once they got the IV in, everyone started rushing toward the operating room. The doctor was walking and saying, "Okay, let's go, let's go." Phillip was on staff, so they let him carry Jay into surgery.

I will never forget watching Phillip walk with Jay toward the operating room. He was holding him close to his chest with his little head up on

---

THAT MAY HAVE BEEN THE FIRST TIME I REALLY TURNED MY LIFE AND THE LIFE OF MY CHILD COMPLETELY OVER TO GOD.

---

his shoulder. And as he walked away from me, all I could see was this tall husband of mine with his big, broad shoulders and this little tiny head peeking up over one of them. My heart was pounding in my chest and I heard myself saying, "Oh my God, what is happening? What's happening to my baby?"

As I stood there, not in the hospital chapel and not in a room but right there in the hall, I gave my child up to God. *Lord*, I prayed, *letting go of that baby is the hardest thing I've ever had to do, but I'm letting him go and turning him over to You. Please hold his little life in Your hands, Lord, and, if it is in Your will, please, please give him back to me. Amen.*

That may have been the first time I really turned my life and the life of my child completely over to God. And as I did it, I felt a burden lift from my shoulders and my heart, because I knew my baby's life was in God's hands. I continued to pray as Phillip and Jay walked farther and farther away, and when they disappeared beyond a set of double doors I sat down for an eternity to wait.

Two hours later, Phillip returned and handed Jay back to me. "He's going to sleep for a while," Phillip said, "but he's fine. He's fine."

Most new parents have had an episode like that, a close call that turned out well but was scary for a while. It stays with you because the feelings it provokes are so powerful that they remain vivid decades later, well after the child is grown. What I remember most clearly about Jay's illness is the fierceness of the feelings I had and how they defined me as a mother. It was my calling to take care of that child; I was his mother, and I believed then as I believe now that I was called by God to love and protect him with every breath I had in me. As strongly as I felt the responsibility of caring and fighting for my child, though, that day in the hospital I knew that part of my responsibility as a mother was to let God take over sometimes.

LIFE LESSON

We are called by God to love
and protect our children with
everything we have; but we are also
called to leave them in His hands.

YOUR TALENT IS GOD'S GIFT TO YOU. WHAT
YOU DO WITH IT IS YOUR GIFT BACK TO GOD.

— *Leo Buscaglia*

God-Given Gifts and Desires

They say that luck is what happens when preparation meets opportunity, and I know it's true. A lot of things seem to go right for me, and it's not because I'm more deserving than other people; it's because I put a lot of energy into making things happen. I'm a great believer in the power of energy—the force that emerges when you set your mind to accomplishing something—and what happens when you use it as a catalyst. Things may not always turn out the way you imagined they would, but that's not the point. The point is to look inside yourself, identify what you need to be happy, and to put things in motion to secure that happiness.

Which is how I came to acquire a Brownie troop.

Phillip was in graduate school and I was working during the day and taking classes at night. We were living in a little house and were not exactly flush; I brought in about $250 a week and Phillip's teaching assistantship netted him about $300 a month, so we didn't go out much. I studied, did things around the house, learned to cook, and took care of us. Phillip and I didn't see all that much of each other because he was studying whenever he wasn't in class; plus, he went away one weekend a month to see patients with his father, who had a thriving psychotherapy practice of his own.

WHEREAS I KNEW WE'D HAVE TO WAIT A FEW YEARS TO HAVE KIDS OF OUR OWN, WHAT WAS TO STOP ME FROM HAVING KIDS AROUND WHO WEREN'T MY OWN?

I have always loved children and was looking forward to having a few of my own. But we barely had enough money to support ourselves and Phillip was adamant about not starting a family until we had more coming in. So, whereas I knew we'd have to wait a few years to have kids of our own, what was to stop me from having kids around who weren't my own?

This is exactly what I had in mind when I picked up the phone and called the local chapter of the Girl Scouts of America and told the woman who answered that I loved little girls and wanted to lead a Brownie troop.

I had to go in for an interview so they wouldn't think I was a lunatic, and I had to prove I really wanted to be a Brownie leader even though

I didn't have any children. And I must have done okay because they said there was a school that needed a leader for a bunch of girls in kindergarten and first grade. They'd let me create and lead a troop as long as I understood that I was on probation, and they'd be checking up to see how I was doing. And I said, "Great!"

I had eight little girls and they would all come to the house and I would run arts and crafts activities. The organization had guidelines we had to follow for the girls to earn their badges, so I did everything just so (I was on probation, after all). At one of our meetings, I remember reading aloud from the official Girl Scout newsletter that kept leaders updated on programs and activities. And I got to the part about the annual Girl Scout jamboree, when they all get together for a few nights and go camping, and these six little girls all started cheering and clapping because they were so excited.

So I'm reading aloud about all the fun they're going to have and I get to the fine print: the overnight camping trip isn't open to Brownie troops. And I stop in the middle of a sentence and say, "Wait a minute, girls, you're too young. We can't do this." And they look up at me with these pitiful faces and they all start to cry. I thought, *Oh, my gosh, what have I done?* It was so pathetic; one minute they were all cheering and the next they were sobbing around my kitchen table. So I said, "Okay, here's the deal; we'll have our own jamboree right here. We'll camp out in my backyard next weekend—how's that?" And don't you know, they were cheering again.

What I didn't realize was that Phillip would be out of town the following weekend, so I would have to run the jamboree on my own. The following Saturday afternoon, eight cars pulled up to the house, and out popped eight little girls with sleeping bags, pillows, and Barbie dolls galore. I had planned all kinds of games and they were having a ball. Our wonderful neighbors Ronnie and Diane helped me feed them; and when it began to get dark, the girls and I piled into our sleeping bags and snuggled up together. I read them stories and we had flashlights and marshmallows, and they eventually got drowsy and fell asleep.

I WAS DRENCHED AND THOUGHT I WOULD KEEL OVER WITH EXHAUSTION. IT WAS ONE OF THE BEST NIGHTS OF MY LIFE.

I did too but was awakened a few hours later by the pitter-patter of raindrops that soon became a deluge. There I was, three o'clock in the morning under a tent with eight groggy girls, and it's lightning and they're squealing and I'm saying, "Girls, we're going to have to go into the house." Their sleeping bags were wet, so I ran to the linen closet, grabbed every sheet and blanket I owned (including the ones off our bed), and made pallets on the floor. Despite my best efforts, two girls were scared to death and crying, so I had to call their parents to come get them in the middle of the night. I was drenched and thought I would keel over with exhaustion. It was one of the best nights of my life.

The next morning dawned bright and clear, and I had six little angels sleeping on the living room floor in my little house; it was just adorable. I loved leading that Brownie troop because I got to do what I love to do: spend time with children and put my energies into making them happy.

I've thought about that Brownie troop many times since I last saw them (those little girls must be well into their thirties by now!), and what tickles me most about the whole experience is that I did it in the first place. I knew very well that troop leaders were typically the mothers of girls in the scouting program, but that didn't stop me. I knew that I wanted to work with children and that I'd have to find a part-time way of doing it. The Girl Scouts seemed like a good match so I pursued them, and we turned out to be perfect for each other.

It's one of the oldest sayings around, but I tend to believe that the Lord helps those who help themselves, and I've never hesitated to help myself to happiness when it's available. And it's available everywhere, if people would only see it.

LIFE LESSON

Look inside yourself, at the goals and dreams God has planted inside you, and identify what you need to be happy, then put things in motion to secure that happiness.

I WOULD RATHER TRUST A WOMAN'S
INSTINCT THAN A MAN'S REASON.

— *Stanley Baldwin*

EMBRACING
the Woman God Created

Men are complex creatures whose ways seem just as mysterious to us as ours do to them. It isn't fair to accuse them of being unromantic or unloving just because their ways of creating romance and expressing love may be different from ours. My point is, don't expect your husband to be like you. Accept him for the man he is, and accept yourself for the woman you are. Do not apologize for your feminine ways. God made you that way on purpose, and don't let anybody tell you there is anything wrong with being a woman and doing things as a woman does them. Women need to be who they are and inspire their husbands to appreciate them as they are. I've always believed that women and men are fundamentally different, that being a feminine woman is just as powerful as being a manly man; and that's something I wish every woman would think about. If your husband makes fun of your feminine ways, tell him to try living without them for a while.

It's always been important for the men in my life to see and respect my femininity and my strength, and to see that my femininity is my strength. When a man and woman are together, the man needs to feel that he's the stronger one in the room, and I don't have a problem with that. Men were put on this earth to stand in the doorway and protect their women and children, and I say, God bless them.

Men have their gifts; we have ours. How many men do you know who pick up on the subtleties of human behavior the way women do? It has nothing to do with intelligence and everything to do with the unique way women perceive things.

ACCEPT HIM FOR THE MAN HE IS, AND ACCEPT YOURSELF FOR THE WOMAN YOU ARE. DO NOT APOLOGIZE FOR YOUR FEMININE WAYS. GOD MADE YOU THAT WAY ON PURPOSE.

It's happened more than once that Phillip and I have been out to dinner with another couple, and something about the way they're looking at each other tells me that something's up with them. In the car going home I'll say, "Phillip, did you notice how they were acting tonight?" And he'll look at me and say, no, he didn't notice anything at all. And then a few days later I run into that woman and she says she's sorry if she and her husband seemed weird that night, but they'd had this little disagreement before they left the house. And I'll go home and in a blaze of triumph tell Phillip what she said; and he'll just look at me as if to say, "And your point is?"

My point is that women are born with gifts of discernment that we could, and should, use to get what we want out of life. But too many of us decline to use our gifts, accepting what comes our way rather than taking charge and making sure that what comes our way is what we want. I cannot count the women I know who feel they've been dealt a crummy hand, yet would rather play the cards they've been given than demand new ones. It's as if they're afraid the Cosmic Dealer will be angry with them if they ask for a better hand.

If you're a woman who is more comfortable reacting to life than acting upon it, I am here to tell you that you get what you ask for and that if you don't ask, you're going to end up settling for less than you want (and deserve).

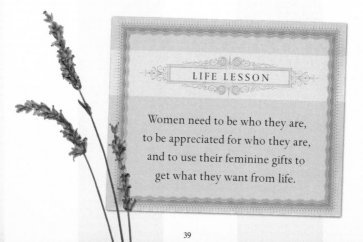

LIFE LESSON

Women need to be who they are,
to be appreciated for who they are,
and to use their feminine gifts to
get what they want from life.

FAITH IS COURAGE; IT IS CREATIVE WHILE
DESPAIR IS ALWAYS DESTRUCTIVE.

— *David S. Muzzey*

Everything

You never know when your life will change forever. One moment your existence is tidy and ordered with everything and everyone in its place; then a tornado blows through and life as you knew it lies scattered around you, tattered and broken and making no sense at all. Sometimes you can see it coming and prepare yourself; other times it's over before you know what hit you and all you can do is stand there, dazed and shell-shocked, and try to make sense of the new reality you must absorb and accept.

That's what happened to me one Sunday morning over twenty years ago when my mother died. I had no warning, no time to prepare. All I had was the sound of her voice and the incomprehensible realization, later, that I would never hear it again. One moment she was talking to me; the next moment there was silence. It was swift and it was final, and I didn't know what hit me—or her—until later.

We got to the hospital, and because Phillip was on staff he was able to get a small private room for us to wait in. I had already called my brother, Roger, and he and his wife showed up shortly after we arrived. I had also called my sisters—Jamie, Karin, and Cindi—who were on their way. Cindi lived a bit of a distance away, so I was worried she might not get there in time to see Mother. They had been particularly close and I knew Cindi would be devastated if she didn't have a chance to say good-bye.

MY FAMILY AND I SAT TOGETHER IN THAT ROOM, FEARING THE WORST YET PRAYING FOR A MIRACLE.

I remember sitting in that little room and telling Phillip, "Go see if she's okay. Go see if she's okay." At the time we did not know that my mother wasn't okay; she had died of a massive heart attack while she was on the phone with me. She was only fifty-eight. My family and I sat together in that room, fearing the worst yet praying for a miracle.

A woman's cry shocked us alert. I ran into the hall and saw Cindi in the waiting room, her coat still on, doubled over and gripping the edge of a molded plastic chair and crying as her heart broke. It was then that I knew my mother was gone. My other sister Karin was with her, silent and stunned. I ran over and asked what had happened. Karin said that she had arrived at the emergency room just as Cindi was walking up to the nurse's station. When Cindi asked, "Where is Mrs. Jameson?"

the nurse replied, "Oh, the woman who died a while ago?" thinking that Cindi was from the funeral home. That's how Cindi learned our mother had died.

I put my arm around Cindi and led her back to the waiting room. We sat down and waited for the reality to sink in. By this time Jamie had arrived and we were all sobbing and holding one another and trying to wrap our minds around the terrible thought that we would never see our mother alive again. I was especially distraught because I had been talking to her when it happened, whining and carrying on about the way my new house smelled all the time she was dying. Every time I thought about her working on the pie she was baking for me while her heart was exploding, I'd break down and start shaking and sobbing all over again. So Phillip quietly stepped out to a pay phone and called his mother to ask her to come down and be with me. She and I were very close (and still are), and he knew it would bring me comfort to have her there.

Fifteen minutes later, Grandma Jerry walked into the room and called my name. And I looked up and cried, "Oh, Grandma, my mother has died! My mother is gone! She's gone!"

That dear, sweet woman took two steps toward me and collapsed with a heart attack.

I am telling the truth.

They rushed Phillip's mother upstairs to the coronary care unit while I watched, stunned and unmoving. The attack was a mild one, and Grandma was soon out of danger. I couldn't help but feel that I was somehow responsible and was shaken by the thought that I'd almost lost two mothers in one day.

I looked down and studied the floor. What world was this? How had I gotten here? I recognized my father and my sisters and my brother and my husband, and yet I knew no one. Everyone looked the same, yet everything was different. My mother was dead and Phillip's mother was in the CCU; it couldn't be and yet it was. What would happen to my father? How would he survive without my mother? What would I do? What would we all do?

NO MATTER HOW ORGANIZED AND VIGILANT WE ARE, FROM TIME TO TIME LIFE STILL HAS A WAY OF BRINGING US TO OUR KNEES.

And something inside me said, *I will survive this . . . I will survive this.* I just knew. I believe that God doesn't give you more than you can handle, and I allowed myself to hold fast to that. I told myself, *Robin, there's a reason for this, and He knows you can handle it.*

As I keep saying, I like to exercise control over my life, and I'm pretty good at it. But my mother's death and other losses since then have taught me that no matter how organized and vigilant we are, from time to time life still has a way of bringing us to our knees. Like it or not, there are some things that cannot be controlled; not by me, not by anyone. Innocent children get hurt, hardworking adults lose their pensions, cities are blown away by hurricanes, and beloved wives, mothers, and grandmothers collapse and die of heart attacks while baking pies for their daughters. You can lament and carry on all you want to, but bad stuff happens to good people and there's not much any of us can do about it except choose how to respond. That is all any of us can do. And ultimately, it's all that matters.

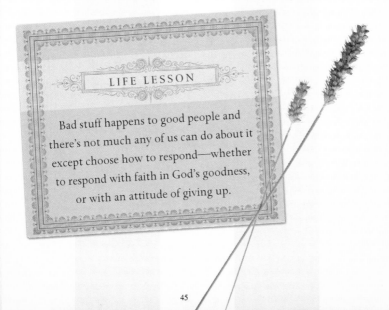

LIFE LESSON

Bad stuff happens to good people and there's not much any of us can do about it except choose how to respond—whether to respond with faith in God's goodness, or with an attitude of giving up.

GOD GAVE US DIFFERENT PASSIONS SO THAT EVERYTHING
HE WANTS DONE IN THE WORLD WILL GET DONE.

— *Rick Warren*

Passion and Purpose

I am in the audience at the *Dr. Phil* show every day, and I have been since it first aired four years ago. I absolutely love it; I wouldn't miss it for the world.

I love being there because this show—the work my husband does in that time—is his life's passion. It is his calling and he has asked me to be there with him and for him. Yes, there are plenty of other things I could do with my time, but none of them means more to me than being in the studio because I share Phillip's passion for this important work.

Phillip will be the first one to tell you that his goal on the show is education, not therapy. Obviously, you can't do psychotherapy in twenty minutes, while breaking for commercials, no less. His hope is that every day people will tune in, see a guest with a problem they can relate to, and maybe get some ideas about how they might deal with it better in their own life. That's the beauty of the show: the people watching it at home can get as much or more out of it than the guests do.

I have great respect for the people who come on the show. I think they are courageous, inspirational, and dedicated to learning how to live a better life. They end up helping not only themselves but a lot of other people as well. Phillip and I both believe that the show is among those that embody the highest and best use of television. He is delivering commonsense information to people's homes every day, free of charge. He never expects people to substitute his judgment for their own, but he does want to make them think. It warms my heart to read the thousands and thousands of letters we receive every month about the changes people are making in their lives because of the show.

I KNOW THAT EVERYTHING PHILLIP HAS DONE IN HIS LIFE UP UNTIL NOW WAS DESIGNED BY GOD TO PREPARE HIM FOR THIS MOMENT.

When Phillip does a show on parenting, for example, we get letters from parents saying things such as, "Until I saw that show, I never realized what I was doing to my children. God bless you for a much-needed wakeup call." I feel really good inside because I know that maybe, just maybe, a small child will get a hug and a kiss that night instead of cruelty and pain. I know that everything Phillip has done in his life up until now was designed by God to prepare him for this moment.

We all have a mission and a purpose in life. I've always felt that being a mother is my calling here on earth. And when the time comes and I'm standing before my heavenly Father, I just want Him to say to me, "Job well done." I feel that when we pursue our callings with passion and intentionality, we see great results in our lives and in the lives of others, and we fulfill our God-given potential.

LIFE LESSON

Whatever we are called to do, we live most fully by pursuing our callings with everything we have within us

GOD HAS ENTRUSTED ME WITH MYSELF.
— *Epictetus*

and Heart

Phillip and I had been dating for almost two years, and although we weren't ready to get engaged, we did want to be together. So I moved out of my parents' house and followed him to Denton when he left for the University of North Texas to start graduate school. I found a small apartment not too far from Phillip's place, and I also found a terrific job as the Unicom operator at Denton Municipal Airport, which meant I gave landing instructions to pilots when they wanted to fly in.

We had been there about a year when I began to feel strongly that I wanted to be married. Phillip and I spent all our nonworking time together, just like a married couple, only we lived in different places. There was no question about our commitment to each other, and it seemed to me that enough time had passed for us both to know what we were getting into. So I took a deep breath one night and put it out there.

"Phillip," I said, "we need to make a decision about where we're going with this. We've been together about three years now, and I would like to get married." He closed his book, cleared his throat, and looked into my eyes.

"Robin," he said, "I can't get married yet. I'm just not ready. I really feel I need to finish my education first. I'm so focused on finishing this program that I don't want to commit to you until I can give 100 percent to being married. I'm not going to get married until I can do that."

I let it sink in for a moment and then I spoke.

"NOW I KNOW HOW YOU FEEL, AND I'M OUT OF HERE." I STACKED UP MY BOOKS, PUT ON MY COAT, AND LEFT.

"You know what?" I said. "I put my cards on the table and you chose not to play the hand. But now I know how you feel, and I'm out of here." I stacked up my books, put on my coat, and left.

It was probably the smartest thing I've ever done.

This was the fall of 1975. I was not quite twenty-two, nor was I quite ready to give up on the idea of marrying Phillip McGraw (just because I broke up with him didn't mean I didn't want him). So I waited a respectable interval after our break-up—about two months—until I knew he was back home for the holidays, and I phoned his parents' house. Phillip and I had not spoken since the night I told him I was out of there, and I knew he had to be missing me. But I didn't want to talk to him just yet. So I picked a time he was likely to be out, called him at his parents' house, and left a message for him to call me. (I may have even been in cahoots with his sister or his mother to find out for certain when he'd be out; I don't remember.) I wanted to call when he wouldn't be there so I could tantalize him with an "I wondered if you could call me" message. I knew he would call back.

And he did. I had my roommate answer even though I was sitting right there—these were the days before caller ID, so I asked her to answer all our phone calls so I wouldn't get caught by surprise. She said, "Oh, sorry. Robin's not here, she's out on a date."

And he said, "Ohhh . . ." I could hear it; I had my ear next to the receiver while she was talking. Then she very politely took a message and hung up.

He called back a few days later and this time I got on the phone. He said, "Hi, you know, I'm coming back from winter break in a couple of weeks and I'm going to be flying in on a Friday night just as you're getting off work. So could we maybe go to dinner and see each other?"

"Sure," I said, just as cool as could be. And he gave me the tail number of his airplane—5902Q (I can't believe I still remember that)—and I hung up the phone. I was so excited, I could not sit down for a good half hour.

So the big night finally came. I was at work at the airport and when he called in from his plane, my roommate turned to me and said, "Here he is, here he is!" And I gave him the landing instructions and saw him taxi in, and he timed it perfectly, just as I was getting off work. We got in the car and went to dinner and then went back to his apartment, where we sat and talked. And we both admitted that we loved each other and missed each other, and that neither of us wanted anybody else.

And he asked me to marry him, and I said yes (big surprise). This was in the middle of January 1976, and a month later, on Valentine's Day, he gave me an engagement ring. We got married six months later to the day, on August 14, 1976.

Not incidentally, I was getting what I wanted. And I had gotten it on my terms.

I BELIEVE THAT GOD MEANS FOR ME TO BE AN ADVOCATE FOR MYSELF, BOTH IN MY MARRIAGE AND EVERY OTHER ASPECT OF MY LIFE.

I have said repeatedly that I believe I was put on this earth to be Phillip's wife and I believe God meant for us to be together. But I also believe that

God means for me to be an advocate for myself, both in my marriage and every other aspect of my life. And no one agrees with me more than Phillip. As he says, we teach people how to treat us, and that night over thirty years ago in his apartment, I taught him that he could not treat me like a comfy old pair of shoes that gathers dust in the closet. I taught him that if we were going to be together, it would have to be on my terms as well as his.

LIFE LESSON

God has created us to serve in many roles, and He has also called us to be an advocate for ourselves in every aspect of life.

FAMILY

IF A WOMAN TRULY LOVES HER FAMILY,
SHE MUST REMEMBER TO LOVE HERSELF.

MOTHERHOOD AT ITS IMPERFECT BEST

THE KEYS TO A MAN'S HEART

FIFTY AND LOVIN' IT—LIFE AFTER KIDS

PERSPECTIVE ON PARENTS

IMAGINE, THEN MAKE IT HAPPEN

TO TAKE CARE OF YOUR FAMILY, TAKE CARE OF YOURSELF

DO WHAT'S RIGHT FOR YOU

CHOOSE FORGIVENESS

PICKING UP ON YOUR MAN'S SIGNALS

THE BEST GIFTS YOU CAN GIVE YOUR HUSBAND

PUTTING HEART INTO YOUR HOME

NEGOTIATING DIFFERENCES

THERE ARE SOME THINGS ONLY A MOTHER CAN DO

I'M ON YOUR SIDE

ONCE YOU ACCEPT THE FACT THAT YOU'RE NOT PERFECT, THEN YOU DEVELOP SOME CONFIDENCE.

— *Rosalynn Carter*

at Its Imperfect Best

I believe I was put on this earth to be not only a wife and a mother, but to be Phillip's wife and Jay and Jordan's mother, and I really just want to be able to look back on my family—my life's work—and know that I did a good job. I have always felt that motherhood was my calling, and I have always known I am going to do everything I can for my children because I want to be able to say that I'm doing a good job, with no regrets.

I want to be proud of myself because I raised decent children. I do not ever want to live with the regret of knowing I could have tried a little harder to help my kids become happy, healthy adults. That doesn't mean I couldn't have done things better or differently. As a young bride and mother, I made all the predictable, typical mistakes and then some. I still cannot believe that I did what I am about to tell you. Talk about a clueless new mother—I defined the term. Okay, here goes.

I brought Jay home from the hospital, placed him in his crib with color-coordinated sheets, blanket, and bumper pads, and realized I didn't have any diapers, bottles, or baby formula in the house. (Heck, I'd only had nine months to prepare, and I was busy decorating the nursery, don't you know?) So I went to the bag of supplies the hospital had sent home with us, fished out the baby bottle and the can of formula, diluted the formula with a can of water the way the hospital nurse had told me to, poured it into the bottle, heated the bottle in a pan of water on the stove, and gave baby Jay his very first home-cooked meal.

THAT DOESN'T MEAN I COULDN'T HAVE DONE THINGS BETTER OR DIFFERENTLY. AS A YOUNG BRIDE AND MOTHER, I MADE ALL THE PREDICTABLE, TYPICAL MISTAKES AND THEN SOME.

In the meantime, I asked Phillip to run to the store and pick up more formula as well as diapers, bottles, and other supplies. It was a good thing he went, because two hours later Jay was ready for his second feeding, right on schedule. I prepared another bottle just as before, fed him, and put him back in his crib.

I barely had time to get comfortable before he was crying for more. That baby sure could eat—it seemed that no more than an hour after finishing a bottle, he'd be hungry again. I was glad Phillip had bought a case of formula, because that child was going through it faster than

I'd gone through pancakes, peanut butter, and watermelon when I was pregnant.

The thing was, Jay didn't seem to be putting on any weight. It didn't make sense: How could a baby eat so much and still look so scrawny? I thought the formula would last us a month, but he was less than a week old, and we were on our last can. So I asked Phillip to run out to the market and get some more. "What's it called again?" he said.

I picked up the last can to look at the label, and my heart lurched.

"Oh, my gosh. Oh, my gosh," I said.

"What's the matter?" he said.

"Oh, Phillip, I can't believe what I've been doing! I've been mixing the formula with water, only it says right here, 'Do not dilute'! The nurse told me the hospital formula was concentrated and had to be diluted. But this kind was already diluted before they put it in the can."

I'd been starving my baby. My precious, firstborn son was a hungry, puny thing because I'd been feeding him watery formula for four days. I felt so horrible, so guilty, and so ridiculous.

Phillip went out for more formula. I must have examined that label fifty times before I fed that formula to Jay—and this time, I got it right. And he finally began putting on weight.

As much as I don't want to admit it (we never do, do we?), there are a few things I wish I'd done differently. And even though I still cringe when I think about my early attempts to feed my baby, at the time I really was doing my best.

I FIRMLY BELIEVE THAT HOW HAPPY MY SONS ARE IS A REFLECTION OF WHO I AM AND HOW WELL I DID MY JOB.

It's always been important for me to know I was doing the best I could at the time I was doing it, even if my best sometimes wasn't all that good. Both Jay and Jordan managed to survive my many mothering mishaps, which is a relief to me. I firmly believe that how happy my sons are is a reflection of who I am and how well I did my job.

No one's perfect. My kids aren't perfect and I'm not perfect. We don't agree about everything, and every once in a while one of them will do something that makes me want to ask what in the heck they were thinking. But I can honestly say that I feel confident that I've done everything I'm capable of doing.

LIFE LESSON

Nobody's perfect; all that matters
is that we do everything we're
capable of doing.

MARRIAGE IS THREE PARTS LOVE AND
SEVEN PARTS FORGIVENESS OF SINS.

— *Langdon Mitchell*

THE KEYS TO
a Man's Heart

Whe hen it comes to women and what's important to them, men just don't ask the right questions.

I found that out the hard way. It happened more than twenty-three years ago, but the memory is as clear as day. It was a Saturday, and I was in the kitchen fixing dinner. Phillip had been out in the garage for about three hours, trying to find the source of a rattling noise in his car. So he comes in, sees I'm in the middle of cooking, and says, "Hey, can you shut this down for a little bit and come out and help me?"

Being the agreeable young wife I was trying to be back then, I said, "Sure, absolutely." I turned off the flame under the skillet and went out to the garage.

The first thing I noticed was my beautiful bath towel lying on the floor behind the car. It wasn't one of those old, raggedy towels you stack in the garage to wash your car. No, this was a cream-colored, 100 percent Egyptian cotton towel with a big, beautiful *M* monogrammed in blue, one of those thirsty-type towels that's just perfect for drinking up all that oil and grease on the garage floor.

I stood there staring at the towel, and Phillip said, "I've been out here all afternoon and I can't find where that noise is coming from. And I'm just wondering if, you know, you would lie down on the towel and let me back the car out over you, and maybe you can hear the rattle from underneath."

I looked at the towel, I looked at the car, and I looked at him. And I said, "You know what? The only rattle I hear is the one in your head if you think I'm lying down on that towel."

So he tried a different approach.

"Well, then," he said, "will you get in the car and help me?"

"Yes, I sure will," I said. "I can do that." So he opened the trunk and put the towel in there.

Well, ladies, I'm embarrassed and ashamed to admit this, but I got in that trunk. I did. I got in and lay down on my beautiful towel.

I'm thinking we're going to run a few feet back and forth in the garage. Phillip starts the engine, backs out into the driveway, enters the cul-de-sac, and starts zooming around in circles—with me hanging on for dear life. He hits a bump, I close the lid on myself, I'm locked in the trunk, and he's still driving in circles. Now I'm screaming, "Phillip, stop the car! Stop the car!"

Finally the car stops. I hear him come around to the trunk but then he has to go back for his keys so he can open the lid. I hear the key in the lock, right near my head, and as the lid springs open, there's my husband with a hopeful look on his face.

Now, I'm going to tell you what he did not say.

He did not say, "Sweetheart, why are you crying?"

———————— ～⌒◈⌒～ ————————

BUT THE MAN WHO PUT ME IN THE TRUNK OF HIS CAR IS THE SAME MAN WHO, FOR OUR TWENTIETH WEDDING ANNIVERSARY, GAVE ME THE MOST WONDERFUL GIFT I HAVE EVER RECEIVED.

He did not say, "Oh, you're bleeding."

He didn't even say, "Oh here, baby, let me help you out."

No, my beloved husband lifted the trunk lid, gazed into my eyes, and said, "Did you hear anything?"

Let's just say that I didn't hear anything, but he sure did.

But the man who put me in the trunk of his car is the same man who, for our twentieth wedding anniversary, gave me the most wonderful gift I have ever received. We had gone to dinner that night and were going to celebrate by spending the night in a beautiful hotel in Dallas. When we got up to the room, he handed me a gift.

It was a book bound in beautiful black leather, and written on the front, in silver embossed letters, was "Twenty-Year Spin." I opened it, and inside were twenty poems that Phillip had written. Each poem reflected a year of our marriage, from August 14, 1976, to that very day, August 14, 1996. Facing each poem was a collage of photographs depicting the major events of that year, starting with snapshots of our wedding showing Phillip in his white tuxedo and me in my wedding dress, and ending with a poem honoring our twentieth year: "If life were a garden and I could walk through again, you're the flower I would pick for another twenty-year spin."

I'll never forget how I felt when I opened that book. I didn't realize he had it in him to write one poem, let alone twenty. Never in a million years would I have imagined he'd do such a thing. After twenty years, he could still surprise me; and now, after thirty years, he is surprising me still.

I've always seen the vulnerable side of men: They are very open, they want to be happy, they want to be loved, and they want to get along. They can also be tender and unexpectedly defenseless, and sometimes need to turn to their women for strength. If you give a man a safe haven to show his soft and gentle side, and let him know you still think he's strong, I think it makes for a perfect relationship.

I KNOW NOW THAT A BIG PART OF MARRIAGE IS NOT WISHING MY HUSBAND WERE MORE LIKE ME, BUT ACCEPTING AND ACTUALLY ENJOYING THE FACT THAT HE ISN'T.

You've got to get beneath the surface to know who a man really is. From the day I met Phillip, I knew he was a dear, loving person. But to this day, when I introduce him to people, a lot of times they say, "Ooh, your husband scares me." And I've got to admit I had a similar reaction for the first few minutes when I met him thirty-five years ago but I quickly saw that he's the most adorable man ever. I've always looked past what a lot of men put out there, and chosen to see them as large-scale boys who just want to be loved. And when you do that, it's not hard at all to make them happy.

And what makes them happy is to be accepted. That is why I have chosen to bring a spirit of acceptance to my relationship with Phillip, and to embrace the differences between us rather than resist them. And that is why I don't think we should judge our husbands too harshly. We have to accept our mates' ways because that's what makes life interesting.

I talk about acceptance a lot, because it's such an important part of what makes our marriage work. I know now that just because Phillip loves me, doesn't mean he's supposed to think the way I do, or act the way I do, or know you're not supposed to put a thirty-five-dollar bath towel on the garage floor (or your wife in the trunk of your car). I know now that a big part of marriage is not wishing my husband were more like me, but accepting and actually enjoying the fact that he isn't.

On the other hand, I have also learned that just because I have chosen to be half of a couple, doesn't mean I have to stop being who God designed me to be: a loving, amiable wife who is her own person, thinks for herself, and knows that there's more to a working marriage than maintaining a monogrammed towel in pristine condition. After all, Phillip thought he was doing the right thing; he did give me a nice clean, thick towel to lie down on.

LIFE LESSON

What makes men happy
is to be accepted.

WHEN MOTHERS TALK ABOUT THE DEPRESSION OF THE EMPTY NEST, THEY'RE NOT MOURNING THE PASSING OF ALL THOSE WET TOWELS ON THE FLOOR, OR THE MUSIC THAT NUMBS YOUR TEETH, OR EVEN THE BOTTLE OF CAPLESS SHAMPOO DRIBBLING DOWN THE SHOWER DRAIN. THEY'RE UPSET BECAUSE THEY'VE GONE FROM SUPERVISOR OF A CHILD'S LIFE TO A SPECTATOR. IT'S LIKE BEING THE VICE PRESIDENT OF THE UNITED STATES.

— *Erma Bombeck*

Life After Kids

My goal from the moment our sons were born was not to raise them to be terrific two-year-olds and fabulous first graders; it was to raise them to be effective, autonomous adults. Phillip often says on the show that parents aren't raising kids, they're raising adults, and I like to think that maybe he got that from me. Because from the day Jay and Jordan were born, I've always believed that my job was to prepare them for that faraway day when they would be on their own.

Now, with Jay working and Jordan in college, that faraway day has come. And let me tell you, that day came *fast*. When they were babies, people would always tell me to enjoy them while they were little, that before I knew it they'd be all grown up and I wouldn't know where the time had gone. And although I believed them, I didn't fully appreciate how quickly my boys would wiggle through my fingers like they used to in the bathtub and turn into the men they've become. If you have a son, you know what I mean: One day he's soft and tender and wrapping his arms around your waist; the next day he hugs you and your nose mashes up against his collarbone. You hug him back and feel how strong he has become, how much bigger he is than you, and you think, *Oh, my, this isn't a boy, this is a man—my little boy, my son, is a man.*

WHAT DID NOT COME TO AN END WAS THE JOY I FELT—AND CONTINUE TO FEEL—AT BEING THEIR MOTHER.

And in that moment, you can start sobbing—or you can stand up tall, unmash your nose, and get on with your life.

It's all about choice. When my boys were about to leave for college, I had a choice and I thought, *This is their time and I want them excited about it. If I sit around and cry and say, "Oh, I'm going to miss you, I don't want you to go,"* that would mean I was making their leaving all about me, and it's not about me; it's about them. I would have felt very selfish if I'd expressed my love by telling them, "Once you leave, I am going to get up every day and cry." What a burden to put on them! They've earned the right to go on and live this new phase in life.

And that's why, if I cried about them leaving, it was always in bed at night or in the bathtub. (I give myself permission to cry day or night in the bathtub, because it's one of my favorite places to be.) My tears were for the joy of being their mother. And of course that came to an end, that daily mothering, when they left for college. But what did not come to an end was the joy I felt—and continue to feel—at being their mother. And that's because I made that conscious choice to celebrate their independence rather than grieve their absence. I chose to rejoice in their competence rather than mourn the fact that they don't need me anymore. Because, in fact, they do still need me, only in different ways than they used to. Just as they have grown and evolved, so have I; and just as they are excited about entering this new phase of their lives, so am I excited about entering this new phase in my life.

It's all a matter of how you look at it: when our kids leave the nest, we can either reject our children's coming of age and pretend they're still little kids who can't live without us, or we can accept that they've grown into the adults we hoped they'd become and get on with our lives.

I choose acceptance.

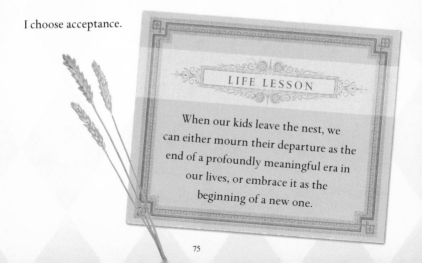

LIFE LESSON

When our kids leave the nest, we can either mourn their departure as the end of a profoundly meaningful era in our lives, or embrace it as the beginning of a new one.

WE ACQUIRE THE STRENGTH WE HAVE OVERCOME.

— *Ralph Waldo Emerson*

Parents

My mother was the sweetest, gentlest woman you could ever meet. She loved being a mother, and I know I get that from her. And my father absolutely adored me, and I adored him. He loved all five of us kids and made each of us feel as if we might just be his favorite. That was the good part of my father.

There was another part too, a part that had to do with him drinking and not coming home and us not knowing where he was, whom he was with, or what he was doing. It didn't seem to go with the rest of him, and yet there it was.

What I learned from reflecting on my parents' legacy is that life is complicated and love does not conquer all. I learned that as much as my father loved me, he wasn't strong enough to save me from his disease; and as much as I adored him, there were aspects of him that I disliked immensely. I learned that I admired my mother's strength, and that one day I would protect my own children the way she protected us. But I also learned that her refusal to acknowledge my father's alcoholism had backfired, and her strategy of pretending nothing was wrong was one that would not work for me. And so I made the choice to embrace those parts of my parents' legacy that were good and wholesome, and to absolutely, categorically reject the rest.

YOU'RE NOT BETRAYING YOUR PARENTS BY LIVING YOUR LIFE DIFFERENTLY THAN THEY LIVED THEIRS; IN FACT, WHAT YOU'RE DOING IS BEING TRUE TO YOURSELF.

The concept of redefining your legacy is something I am passionate about, especially when it comes to women, many of whom are merely existing inside lives they neither chose nor contemplated. So many of us have dutifully reproduced our mother's or father's behaviors, duplicating our parents' patterns and manifesting a legacy that we, however unconsciously, feel obligated to fulfill.

I want you to know you have a choice: you do not have to haul your parents' legacy into your life like that old dining room set your great aunt left for you in her will. If it makes you happy to eat at that table and sit in those chairs, by all means keep them. But if it doesn't, remember: you have options. You can hold on to the table and toss the chairs. Or lose the table and keep the chairs (perhaps reupholster the seats so they're more comfortable). And if you just plain hate the whole thing, get rid of it before you bring it into the house.

Just as your great aunt's furniture might not suit your dining room, your parents' ways of living might not suit your life. You're not insulting your dead aunt by rejecting her old furniture, and you're not betraying your parents by living your life differently than they lived theirs; in fact, what you're doing is being true to yourself. I believe in the core of my being that you don't have to bring into your life anything that isn't working for you, nor are you fated to live out a future you had no part in creating. Each of us possesses the will to create our own legacy. It's all a choice.

LIFE LESSON

If we want to be truly autonomous, truly our own selves, and take our lives to the next level, we must embrace the good parts of our upbringing and refuse to allow the bad parts to rule our lives.

IF YOU DON'T KNOW WHERE YOU ARE GOING,
YOU WILL PROBABLY END UP SOMEWHERE ELSE.

— *Lawrence J. Peter*

Then Make It Happen

As I grew up, I dedicated my life to undoing the legacy of doubt, fear, and pain that accompanied my father's great love for us. My father taught me how good it felt to be really loved, and I vowed that when I had children someday, they would also feel really loved. But I also vowed to raise my children without the terrible uncertainty I grew up with. I promised myself that any children I brought into this world would grow up feeling not only loved but also supported by a consistent level of certainty that I never had as a child.

I am happy to say I have kept that promise, and I kept it both by the grace of God and the gift of free will. I kept this promise to my children by vowing not to marry a man who drank or gambled. And the fact that my children's father doesn't drink or gamble isn't a matter of chance, it's a matter of choice. It's no accident that Phillip embodies the values I wanted for the father of my children; the only reason he's the father of my children is because he embodies those values, and did when we were dating. That's why I chose him, and that's why I wanted him to choose me. I am certain he had similar standards that I met as well.

IT'S NO ACCIDENT THAT PHILLIP EMBODIES THE VALUES I WANTED FOR THE FATHER OF MY CHILDREN; THE ONLY REASON HE'S THE FATHER OF MY CHILDREN IS BECAUSE HE EMBODIES THOSE VALUES.

I keep coming back to this issue of making choices because I know so many people who don't realize they have the right to choose how they live, people who would be so much happier if only they would examine the connection between what they do and how their lives turn out. They think their lives are predetermined, that things will always fall short of their expectations because that's just the way things go for them. They tell me that I'm different from them, that I'm so lucky, that I have the perfect life, the perfect marriage, and the perfect house.

Well, guess what? Nothing is perfect. I'm not, my marriage isn't, Phillip isn't, our kids aren't, and the house isn't (although there is one room that comes close). When it looks as if people have all this great stuff going on, it's only because it's right for them, and that's because they did their best to make it that way. As for being lucky, forget about it.

It's not about luck; it's about figuring out what you want and making it happen.

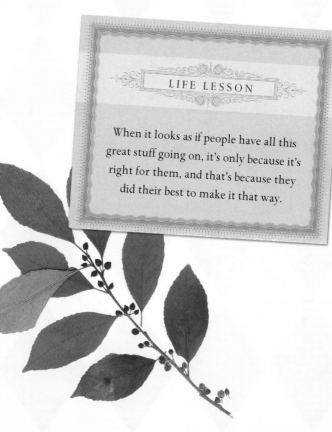

LIFE LESSON

When it looks as if people have all this great stuff going on, it's only because it's right for them, and that's because they did their best to make it that way.

TO BE IN YOUR CHILDREN'S MEMORIES TOMORROW,
YOU HAVE TO BE IN THEIR LIVES TODAY.

— *Barbara Johnson*

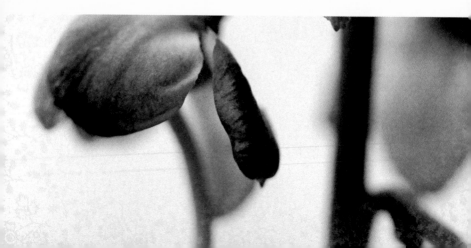

Take Care of Yourself

I n the days that followed my mother's burial, I replayed the events surrounding her death over and over in my mind. First it made me cry, and then it made me think.

I was thirty-one years old, married for eight years, and the mother of a six-year-old boy. There was nothing in the world as precious to me as my husband and son. Just as my mother had always put her family's needs before her own, I had put my family's needs before mine. Like most mothers, I daydreamed about the milestones to come in Jay's life, and pictured myself beaming beside him as he grew stronger and taller and took his place in the world. In my mind I was always there, smiling and protecting him and making sure he was happy, just as my mother always did for us . . .

And then it would hit me. She was gone.

I was a mother and my own mother was dead. My young son would grow up without his grandmother and perhaps forget what she looked like, or even that she existed. My life was immeasurably, profoundly diminished because she was gone. And she was gone because she didn't take care of herself.

I REALIZED THAT MY MOTHER HAD MARTYRED HERSELF FOR THE SAKE OF HER FAMILY, AND WE WERE ALL THE POORER FOR IT.

It was then that I realized that loving your family and neglecting yourself are not the same thing; that, in fact, if a woman truly loves her family, she must not and will not neglect herself. It was the same kind of revelatory moment I had as a teenager, when I realized that my father was a drunk. This time, I realized that my mother had martyred herself for the sake of her family, and we were all the poorer for it.

When I thought of her baking that pie—the pie I'd asked her to make—while she was having a heart attack, I felt as if my own heart would crack with grief. The thought of it sitting on the stove, cold and uneaten in that lonely house, hurt me so much I asked Phillip to drive over there before the funeral and throw it away. Under no circumstances could I bear to walk into that house and see it.

It seems strange when I think about it now: That pie was the last thing my mother touched. She made it out of love for me. Yet after she died, I could not bear the thought of even looking at it. Why? Why did it not seem even more precious after she was gone? Why did I not want to taste it and remember her wonderful baking? Why did I not choose to freeze it as people do a slice of their wedding cake, to preserve the memory of the love it signified?

The reason, I believe, is that the pie became for me a symbol of the colossal self-neglect that had taken my mother's life. I could not bear to look at it, let alone taste it, because it was the thing she was paying attention to when she should have been paying attention to herself.

IT WAS TOO LATE TO PERSUADE HER TO TAKE BETTER CARE OF HERSELF, BUT IT WASN'T TOO LATE FOR ME TO LEARN FROM HER TRAGEDY AND VOW TO TAKE CARE OF MYSELF.

I realized that it was too late to persuade her to take better care of herself, but it wasn't too late for me to learn from her tragedy and vow to take care of myself.

And I do. Ever since my mother died, I take care of myself as if my life depended on it. I do a breast self-exam in the shower several times a month. I go to the dentist every six months and have my teeth cleaned and checked. Every year I get a complete physical, a mammogram, and a Pap smear. And pardon me if I get on a soapbox here, ladies, but I'm talking to you. If you have not seen a doctor in the last year, please, please take a moment to think about yourself, about the gift of life that God has given you, and how little time it takes for you to protect that gift. If you're not convinced, think about the people who love you—your husband, your children, your parents—and think about what their lives would be like without you. That's precisely the process I went through when my mother died: I pictured Jay having to grow up without me and Phillip having to raise him without me. I vowed I would always, always take care of myself—if not for my sake, then for theirs.

LIFE LESSON

If you want to be around to take care
of your family, you have to devote
time to taking care of yourself.

EVERYTHING IS SOMETHING YOU DECIDE TO DO,
AND THERE IS NOTHING YOU HAVE TO DO.

— *Denis Waitley*

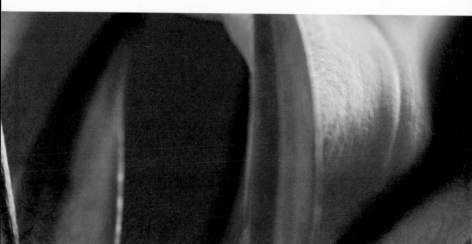

DO WHAT'S RIGHT
for You

O ne of the reasons our marriage works so well is that we talk. We have always talked. We talked before we got married about what we expected from each other, and what we could and could not live with.

If you watch Phillip's show, you have probably heard him say that we teach people how to treat us, and you can be sure that I taught him exactly how to treat me. And he's been a superb student. He is also an experienced teacher because, as it turned out, I also had a thing or two to learn.

When I was growing up and my father said something I didn't like, I pouted, and then I usually got what I wanted. I'd sulk and I wouldn't talk and I wouldn't look at him, and he just hated that, so sooner or later, I got my way. This worked well for me, and I stashed it in my collection of viable relationship techniques. Then, years later when I was dating Phillip, he said something once that I wasn't crazy about. I don't recall what it was, but I do recall that it bothered me, so I got all quiet and pensive; I probably even stuck out my lower lip. This went on for a while, maybe even a couple of days, before Phillip sat me down for a chat.

"You've got to know right now," he said, "that I can't put up with pouting. If I've done something, just tell me. If I ever do anything to upset you, promise that you'll just come and tell me what I've done, because if you tell me what I did, I can tell you right now, I will never do it again."

That sounded good, so I said fine, and told him he should do the same with me. But I'd never had to do that before, and it took me a while to muster the courage to tell him the truth. But I finally said, "Well, okay, fine. The other day you said something that really hurt my feelings." And he said, "Okay, I'm sorry. I won't say that anymore."

But what if he hadn't said that? What if he had told me to lighten up and learn to get over my hurt feelings? What if he had told me that he loved me but couldn't promise me that he would never stay out all night drinking, or never place a bet on a horse?

I would have moved on, that's what. Oh, yes, I would.

As much as we love our men, the one thing we need to love even more is ourselves. Only we can know what we need to do to survive, to flourish, and harnessing ourselves to someone who brings chaos into our lives is not it. We are worthy; we are worth being loyal to; we are worth our men saying, "Yes, you are the most important person in my life."

AS MUCH AS WE LOVE OUR MEN, THE ONE THING WE NEED TO LOVE EVEN MORE IS OURSELVES.

As much as I wanted to marry Phillip, it wasn't about me holding on to him at any cost; it was about me holding on to me. I always wanted to be the most important part of my husband's life, whomever I married. If it wasn't going to be Phillip McGraw, it would be someone else. And whomever it was, no one and nothing would be more important to him than I was.

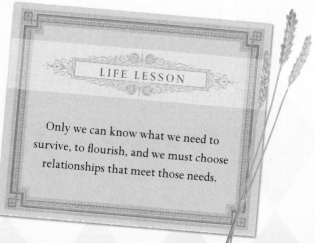

LIFE LESSON

Only we can know what we need to survive, to flourish, and we must choose relationships that meet those needs.

A HAPPY MARRIAGE IS THE UNION
OF TWO GOOD FORGIVERS.

— *Ruth Bell Graham*

CHOOSE

Forgiveness

Many people reached out to me in the wake of my mother's death. They brought food, they brought flowers, they called, they sent cards; most of all, they reminded me that even though my mother was gone I was far from alone in the world, and it touched me deeply. When my mother was buried and everyone went home, I told Phillip that it was important for me to sit down and write thank-you notes to everyone who had come to honor my mother's memory. I wanted to let them know how much their affection meant to me, and I wanted to do it while the feelings were still fresh. And Phillip said, "Absolutely."

For four days I sat at the dining room table writing notes and letters, every one by hand. I thanked people for reaching out to me and then would cry and sob as I wrote about my mother and told them about how wonderful she was. It was a therapeutic experience for me because I got to think about my mother in the context of all these people she had known. It gave me a chance to think about her not only as my mother but as a friend, neighbor, relative, and colleague of many other people, all of whom had known her in a different way than I had. I would sit there until I was all cried out; then I'd go to bed and start again the next morning.

I FELT DEVASTATED AND SHOCKED AND SAD AND ANGRY.

I finally finished the notes. I put a stamp on each one, stacked them up, put them in a little bag, handed them to Phillip, and said, "If you'll mail these for me tomorrow at the office, I can now start living my life without my mother." And he took the bag and said, "Of course I will."

One morning about three weeks later while Phillip was in the shower, I picked up his tennis bag and swung it onto the bed. Phillip was in private practice at the time, and at the end of the day he would stop and play tennis before coming home. I would typically get the bag ready for him and put in his tennis shoes, tennis shorts, clean socks, and a T-shirt, and he'd take it to work with him. I realized that I hadn't done it in a while and felt like getting back into my old routine.

I gathered up his tennis clothes and was putting them into the bag when I felt something bulging in from a side pocket. And I thought, *Ugh, I bet that sweaty shirt has been in there since the last time I emptied this thing.* I unzipped the pocket and reached down in there, and what did I find but the bag full of thank-you notes.

My heart broke. It was as if my mother had died all over again.

I started crying. As I stood there weeping and missing my mother, Phillip walked into the room. He stared at me and he stared at those notes and he stood there with the most horrified look on his face.

"Oh . . . my . . . God," he said, his voice barely a whisper. "I forgot to mail them." I was really sobbing now.

"I thought they knew! I thought they knew! I've seen these people, Phillip, in the store, and on the street, and I never said a word of thanks to them because I thought they'd gotten my cards! I thought they knew!" The poor man just stood there. His face was the color of ashes.

I was hurt, I was angry, I was in pieces all over again. Not only had I felt good about thanking so many people for comforting me, but writing to them about my mother and imagining them reading what I'd written was a huge part of my healing process. I had seen these people around town, and it had given me comfort to know that there had been an exchange between us, that I had properly acknowledged their condolences, expressed my gratitude for their caring, and left them knowing a little bit more about my mother after her death than they had known when she was alive. When I'd see these people in town I would think, *We are some of the lucky ones, you and I, because we share this secret of how extraordinary my mother was, and how great a loss it is that she is gone.*

But now that illusion was also gone; there was no knowledge between us, no secret shared. I felt like one of those palm trees you see on Weather Channel hurricane updates, blasted about by gale-force emotional winds that could blow me over at any moment. I felt devastated and shocked and sad and angry.

I also felt betrayed: *Here I believed you thought it was important for me to sit and write these notes—you told me you did—so how could you forget?* That was the crux of it: How could this matter so little to him? How could this man think he knew me and not realize the value of these notes? How could he think he loved me if he couldn't remember to do this one hugely important thing?

I looked up and Phillip was standing in the same place quietly saying, "I'll cancel my patients and I'll spend the whole day . . . I'll call them . . . I'll make a list and call them. I'll get their phone numbers, I'll call everyone—no, I'll go see them, that's what I'll do, I'll hand-deliver the notes. Just give them to me and I'll go right now, Robin, I'll do whatever it takes. Please, please let me make this up to you."

And something melted inside me and I thought, *Bless his heart. This precious man is devastated, just as I am*, and suddenly I knew that his feelings were more important to me than the feelings of the people who hadn't received the notes. I thought, *He is suffering so much more for not mailing the notes than they are for not receiving them; what do I gain by punishing him with my anger? What benefit do I derive from making him suffer more?*

This was a powerful moment for me personally and a pivotal one in our marriage. At that moment, I had the opportunity to show this man who I really was, this man who had told me years ago, "People have the right to think and say and do whatever they want to. And you have the right to choose not to react."

THIS WAS A POWERFUL MOMENT FOR ME PERSONALLY AND A PIVOTAL ONE IN OUR MARRIAGE. AT THAT MOMENT, I HAD THE OPPORTUNITY TO SHOW THIS MAN WHO I REALLY WAS.

I had the right to rant and rave and scream and yell and make Phillip feel horrible. *I had the right to behave that way, but that's not who I am.* Instead, I seized the opportunity to show him who I actually was: a compassionate and forgiving woman who loved him, no matter what, who would forgive him, no matter what.

So I looked into his sad, sad eyes and blotted my own with my sleeve. "I know you didn't do it on purpose," I said. "We'll mail them today and they'll get them tomorrow. I love you and I know you love me, and I know you didn't do it on purpose." And the look of gratitude on his face showed how fortunate he felt. I think of that moment as the one when Phillip learned that my love for him and commitment to him were stronger than any mistake he might make. I believe that was the moment he learned he could trust me, and he has never forgotten it.

Nor have I forgotten what I learned that day about the nature of love and mercy and forgiveness and their role in a working marriage.

I believe in forgiveness. I believe that, just as God promises to forgive us, He wants us to forgive one another. Every day offers a chance to choose either anger or understanding, bitterness or acceptance, darkness or light. And the choices we make reveal the stuff we're made of.

LIFE LESSON

Every day offers a chance to choose
either anger or understanding,
bitterness or acceptance,
darkness or light.

THE AVERAGE MAN IS MORE INTERESTED IN
A WOMAN WHO IS INTERESTED IN HIM THAN
HE IS IN A WOMAN WITH BEAUTIFUL LEGS.

— *Marlene Dietrich*

Man's Signals

M en are different from us; they're not going to take us by the hand and say, "Sweetheart, I want to talk to you about these feelings I've been having," and beg us to do this, that, or the other thing—forget that. What they are going to do is get out of the shower twenty minutes before you're due to be somewhere and say, "So, what are you thinking of wearing tonight?" It doesn't matter that your outfit is laid out on the bed alongside seven others you've already rejected and they're all long, dressy, and black. Because he's not really asking you what you're going to wear, he's asking you to tell him what he's going to wear. It's a guy code they use to let us know that they need help without actually asking for it. That way, they get their needs met without having to admit to us that they actually have needs in the first place.

But men do have needs, of course, and all things considered, they're pretty good about putting the information out there for us to find.

Which is why I'm astonished at the number of women who either don't pick up the signals their men are sending out or, even worse, pick them up loud and clear and choose to ignore them, as though it would diminish their power to help out.

YOU DON'T HAVE TO BE A MIND READER TO FIGURE OUT WHAT YOUR MAN WANTS AND NEEDS TO BE HAPPY; HE'LL LAY IT RIGHT OUT THERE.

I once knew a woman who was always at odds with her husband. They didn't argue or yell, but it was as if she had a constant, underlying need to get him before he got her. I couldn't figure it out; I never heard him speak unkindly or disrespectfully to her, and he seemed like a very decent man. Still, his happiness was never very high on her list of priorities.

I remember she was at the house once when her husband was away on a fishing trip and she was talking about how he loved to meet up with these old friends every year, and they would rent a boat and spend a week hanging out and being guys together. She said he had been gone a week and was coming home that afternoon. I looked at the clock and saw that it was past three o'clock.

"You'd better get going," I said, "or you won't be there when he gets back."

"Oh, that's okay," she said.

"But don't you want to be there when he gets home?"

"No, not really."

"What?"

"Sure, he'd like me to be sitting there when he gets home so he can drag in the cooler and show me all the fish he caught. If he's so interested in being with me, why does he need to go away? If he's going to go away for a week, fine, but I'm sure as heck not going to be sitting there when he walks in, because that's exactly what he wants."

Was she kidding me? He's telling her what he wants, what he needs, what he likes, and she's not going to do it on purpose?

IF YOUR MATE LETS YOU KNOW WHAT HE WANTS AND YOU USE THAT INFORMATION TO HURT HIM, YOU HAVE TO ASK YOURSELF WHY YOU ARE IN THE RELATIONSHIP IN THE FIRST PLACE.

What's up with that?

If your mate lets you know what he wants and you use that information to hurt him, you have to ask yourself why you are in the relationship in the first place. Here's this woman doing the opposite of what her husband wants so he won't think he can control her, whereas if she would wait for him to come home, crawl up in his lap, and flirt with him, she'd have him hooked better than anything in that cooler of his.

You don't have to be a mind reader to figure out what your man wants and needs to be happy; he'll lay it right out there. That's the thing about men: they may not like to talk about their feelings, but they're usually direct about making their feelings known.

LIFE LESSON

Men may not like to talk about their feelings, but they're usually direct about making their feelings known.

THE HOME SHOULD BE A WARM SANCTUARY FROM THE STORMS OF LIFE FOR EACH MEMBER OF THE FAMILY. A HAVEN OF LOVE AND ACCEPTANCE. NOT ONLY CHILDREN, BUT ALSO PARENTS, NEED THIS SECURITY.

— *Anonymous*

THE BEST GIFTS YOU CAN GIVE

Your Husband

There's one thing I know about men: they love to know that their women appreciate them. Sometimes the best gift you can give your man is the reassurance that his happiness means something to you. It's good to remember that men have feelings, even though they do their best to hide them.

One Christmas morning many years ago I was opening a gift from Phillip and looked up to see him watching me. He had that look on his face that a man gets when he's done something special for his wife and he can't wait to see her reaction. I tore off the wrapping, lifted the lid, and with a cry of joyful surprise, held up the contents for the whole family to see. It was a black suede bomber jacket decorated with fringe across the front, back, and cuffs and embroidered with red and blue crystal beads and glistening, iridescent sequins.

It was striking, unique, beautifully made, and I didn't like it. I turned to

Phillip and he was beaming just the way Jordan and Jay did when they gave me Mother's Day cards they had made themselves. And I thought, *He's so proud at having picked this out for me. He must have thought, "I'm going to buy her something to wear," and he picked out this jacket and he wants to see me in it, and, oh my gosh, I don't like it.* But I would never tell him that.

THERE'S ONE THING I KNOW ABOUT MEN: THEY LOVE TO KNOW THAT THEIR WOMEN APPRECIATE THEM.

"Hey!" he said, his face bright and expectant. "Do you like it?"

"Oh, honey, this is a beautiful gift!" I said, and I threw my arms around him and hugged him. And the fact is, the jacket was beautiful in its own way, if for no other reason than that Phillip had bought it and wanted so much for me to like it.

I displayed the jacket prominently all day and hung it in my closet that night. On several occasions after that, when Phillip called me from the tennis court to tell me he was on his way home, I put on the jacket as if I had worn it that day. And when he walked in from work there I was, wearing the jacket, and his face lit up and I knew I had made him happy. I never said anything about it because I thought that would be too obvious; I just wore it . . . but never out of the house. The challenge was to find a way of showing my husband that I loved what the jacket symbolized even if I didn't love the jacket itself.

Now, if you're thinking that I wasn't being exactly honest with Phillip about my feelings that Christmas morning, you're right: I was being genuine, not honest, because to be totally honest would have meant being brutal and hurting his feelings. I have to tell you: if I had to do it over, I wouldn't change a thing. Sparing Phillip's feelings that morning was far more important than being honest with him about how I felt about the jacket, because doing so gave my husband the gift of appreciation.

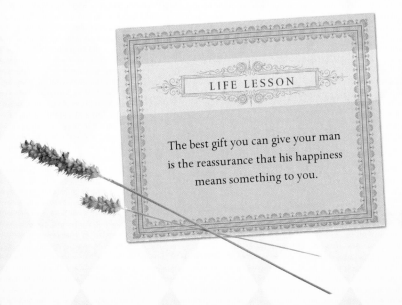

LIFE LESSON

The best gift you can give your man is the reassurance that his happiness means something to you.

A HOME IS A HOUSE WITH A HEART INSIDE.

— *Author Unknown*

PUTTING HEART INTO

Your Home

Like everyone else, I am not one person but many. I am a daughter to parents no longer living; a sister to four adults who bear scars, as I do, of growing up in a loving but chaotic household. I am a wife to a man whose heart I hold in my hands; and a mother to sons whose lives I hold dearer than my own. I am a sister-in-law, a daughter-in-law, and I am soon to have a daughter-in-law of my own. And above all those things and embracing all things, I am the heart of my home.

Aren't all women the hearts of their homes? Whether we live alone or in a household spanning three generations, whether we work outside the home as well as within it or stay at home full-time, it's the women who make sure there's food in the fridge, curtains on the windows, sheets on the beds, and a hug for whoever needs it. With few exceptions, it's a woman's spirit that brings a house its warmth, brightens its shadowy corners, and provides those who live there with a soft place to fall. There are as many ways to do this as there are women: we all have our own unique way of being in this world and creating the joy and warmth that make a house a home.

IT'S THE WOMEN WHO MAKE SURE THERE'S FOOD IN THE FRIDGE, CURTAINS ON THE WINDOWS, SHEETS ON THE BEDS, AND A HUG FOR WHOEVER NEEDS IT.

I have always chosen to cultivate a spirit of happiness in our home. It didn't get there by itself; I made it that way. It is not enough that I am happy in myself; I choose to spread a spirit of joy and fun to the family. If I don't, Phillip and the boys might not have it, and it's exactly what they need.

If I weren't around, my husband would probably work all the time, and he's not the only one: I often hear women talking about how their husbands have forgotten how to leave work behind, let go, and have fun. A lot of these are working women, so they understand how difficult it is to juggle professional and personal responsibilities. Still, they seem to be better at making time for fun than their husbands, and are at a loss as to how to help their husbands do the same. I know what it's like to be married to a man who loves to work, and I'd like to pass along something I've learned: one of the best things women can do to make their husbands happy is to be happy themselves. Phillip cannot stand it if he thinks I'm unhappy about something, and I know it brings a real peace to his life—and to our household—to know that I am just where I want to be, doing just what I want to do.

I like to try to make everything fun for my family. When the boys were little and Phillip and I were going out of town—Phillip traveled a lot to do seminars, and sometimes I would go with him—we would leave them with their grandparents, who spoiled them rotten. Still, just to make sure they didn't miss us too much, I would get little bags and if we were going to be gone Monday, Tuesday, and Wednesday, I'd write "Monday a.m.," "Monday p.m.," and so on. I'd put a little note in along with something fun—a Hot Wheels car, a piece of gum, a sucker, whatever they loved—and they'd get to open them when they woke up in the morning and before they went to bed. That was my way of letting them know that there were times when Mom and Dad needed to go away together, but that we were always loving them and thinking of them.

I also made a big deal about holidays. In spring, I would buy little napkins decorated with Easter eggs and chicks, write a message on the napkin, and stick it in their lunch boxes so they'd get a loving note from me while they were at school. Every Valentine's Day I would buy red heart-shaped balloons and tie them to their chairs before they came down for breakfast. On their birthdays I took lipstick and wrote messages on their bathroom mirror while they were sleeping, so they'd wake up, go in to brush their teeth, and get a surprise.

I would often try to find ways to surprise them. On the days Jay had a game after school, I would drive out there and take him a hot lunch because the school he went to had no kitchen, and he'd get hungry during the game if he hadn't had a substantial lunch. I would serve the boys' favorite dinner on game days, and surprise them with their favorite dessert. Sometimes I'd bake a chocolate-chip cookie cake (get rolled-up cookie dough, press it into a pan, and, presto!), put their jersey number on it in M&Ms, and let them have it when we got home from the game. They loved that because not only did it make game days feel special to them, it let them know that I thought they were special too.

And I think that's what being the hearts of our homes is all about: making our families feel thought about and cared for.

We all have our own unique way
of creating the joy and warmth
that make a house a home.

WHEN WE REALLY LOVE OTHERS, WE ACCEPT THEM AS THEY ARE. WE MAKE OUR LOVE VISIBLE THROUGH LITTLE ACTS OF KINDNESS, SHARED AC-TIVITIES, WORDS OF PRAISE AND THANKS, AND OUR WILLINGNESS TO GET ALONG WITH THEM.

— *Edward E. Ford*

NEGOTIATING

Differences

I believe that good marriages aren't born, they're made—and they're made over time by an ongoing process of loving, unselfish negotiation. It's funny—people are forever asking me how Phillip and I have managed to be married for thirty years and still be happy. They think we have some sort of mysterious secret; when I tell them we've done it by negotiating our differences, they look almost disappointed. "Negotiate?" they say. "That sounds so, so . . . unromantic."

Well, hello! Who ever said marriage is romantic? Marriage is about partnership, sharing, cooperation, and compromise. Sure, romance is in there too, but it tends not to surface unless the other components are in place. And they're not going to fall into place easily and peacefully all the time. Sometimes you have to advocate for yourself in a relationship, which means figuring out what your needs are in a given situation and having the conviction to be honest with your partner about it.

Here's an example. One weekend while Phillip was in graduate school, my sister Cindi invited me to spend the weekend at her house. So I called Phillip and told him that I was going to visit my sister for the weekend and I invited him to come along. We weren't married yet, and, between his classes, studying, and teaching-assistant job, I didn't see him that much. So I thought it would be fun to hang out with my sister and nieces for a few days. And he said, "Sure, I'll go."

MARRIAGE IS ABOUT PARTNERSHIP, SHARING, COOPERATION, AND COMPROMISE. SURE, ROMANCE IS IN THERE TOO, BUT IT TENDS NOT TO SURFACE UNLESS THE OTHER COMPONENTS ARE IN PLACE.

About an hour later he called back. "I got to thinking," he said, "and you know what? I am so busy and there's so much I can be doing here, and it's not my thing to sit around and visit and have girl time. I know you want to have a visit with Cindi, so why don't you go by yourself and I'll stay behind?"

And I said, "See you Monday."

Sure, it would have been great if he'd said he wanted to spend the weekend with Cindi and the kids. But the truth was, he didn't. I'll always be grateful to him for being honest about what he wanted to do, because in so doing, he liberated me to be honest about my preferences too. And I have been, throughout our marriage.

Just because Phillip and I came together as a couple doesn't mean that we love all the same things. I never understand it when I hear a woman say she's not going to do something she enjoys because her husband won't do it with her, because that means you have to give up part of yourself for as long as you're married. As I said earlier, you're not the same person as your husband; why expect him to like all the same things you do? I love girl time. I love spa days. Phillip wouldn't go to a spa for the day if you held a gun to his head, but he encourages me to do it (go to the spa, not hold a gun to his head). He is supportive of anything I want to do that brings me joy, and I am supportive of anything he does that brings him joy.

> ### LIFE LESSON
>
> Good marriages aren't born, they're made—and they're made over time by an ongoing process of loving, unselfish negotiation.

WHAT FAMILIES HAVE IN COMMON THE WORLD
AROUND IS THAT THEY ARE THE PLACE WHERE PEOPLE
LEARN WHO THEY ARE AND HOW TO BE THAT WAY.

— *Jean Illsley Clarke*

Only a Mother Can Do

Over the years, I have often chosen to defer to Phillip's judgment when it came to raising our boys. As a man and as a father of sons, it was his job to teach his sons how to be men and fathers, and only he could do it, not I. Both Jay and Jordan were likely to head up families someday, and I saw Phillip instilling in them the drive and commitment it takes to stand in the doorway and protect a wife and children. It was a priority for us to teach our boys what it meant to be responsible, mature men, and a big part of that was teaching them respect for women.

I had the perfect opportunity to teach Jay that respect when he was fifteen. He was a sophomore at an all-boys high school and their all-girls sister school was hosting a big dance that weekend. A girl named Christy, whom he'd met at a previous school function, had invited him to escort her to the dance, which was a couple of days away. Jay was studying for finals when I heard the phone ring; then I heard him saying, "Hello. Oh, hi. Oh, okay. Not really, no, I can't talk right now, I'm studying. Well then, see you." He sat back down with his books and I casually walked by.

IT WAS A PRIORITY FOR US TO TEACH OUR BOYS WHAT IT MEANT TO BE RESPONSIBLE, MATURE MEN, AND A BIG PART OF THAT WAS TEACHING THEM RESPECT FOR WOMEN.

"Who was that?" I said.

"It was Christy."

"What did she want?"

"She called to see if I had any questions about the dance and talk about the color of her dress or something. You know, I wish I didn't even have to go." He was annoyed that she had interrupted him, and I knew I had to set him straight.

"Jay, honey, let me tell you something about girls," I said. "First of all, Christy has spent a lot of time getting ready for this dance. She thought long and hard before she decided whom she wanted to go with her; she picked you, and she's very excited about that. She's spent a lot of time choosing her dress and planning how she's going to wear her hair.

You're her guest, and now she's called to tell you the color of her dress—probably to help you pick out a matching corsage—and you act like you don't even want to go with her. That's not fair. In fact, it's rude.

"You need to call her back right now and show her you're excited about this dance. You need to show her the respect she deserves for choosing you to go with her. Because I guarantee you that she is not feeling very happy right now.

"And Jay, let me tell you something else about women: when it comes to men, women never forget. If I were you, I'd be nice to this girl because someday, she just might own the company you want to work for. And I promise you when you walk in for your interview, she will remember how you treated her, and you don't want to lose a job when you're thirty because you didn't act like a gentleman when you were fifteen.

I WANTED JAY TO KNOW THAT IT WASN'T ENOUGH TO TREAT HER WITH RESPECT; HE ALSO HAD TO TREAT HER WITH COMPASSION.

"And let me tell you something else: girls talk. If you don't treat her right, she'll tell all her friends how mean and rude you are. And they'll think twice before they ask you to be their date, or agree to go out with you if you ask them.

"You agreed to escort this girl to her dance, and you should do it with pride. And even if you never want to go out with her again, you should still be her friend. Because afterward, you want her to tell her friends, 'No, we're not dating anymore, but let me tell you something, girls—he is the nicest guy, and I will always be his friend.' Don't ever forget that, Jay. Trust me—I'm a woman, and I know."

I had said my piece. Jay went to the phone, called Christy back, and said all the things he should have said the first time.

There are certain things that only a woman can do, and one of them is teaching her son about women. I wanted Jay to know that it wasn't enough to treat a woman with respect; he also had to treat her with compassion.

There are certain things that only a woman can do, and one of them is teaching her son about women.

LOVE COMES WHEN WE TAKE THE TIME TO
UNDERSTAND AND CARE FOR ANOTHER PERSON.
— *Janette Oke*

I'M

on Your Side

It's not always easy to see things from your partner's point of view; but it's something I've consistently tried to do in my marriage. If Phillip and I get along well, it's not because we agree on everything; it's because we both make an effort to understand why the other is thinking, feeling, or acting a certain way. After thirty years, you get to know a man pretty well, and I know that if Phillip and I aren't seeing eye to eye, it's not because he isn't looking at the situation carefully. It's because he's seeing it differently than I am.

Years ago, I knew a woman who lived in a big, beautiful house that I absolutely loved. It was high up on a hill and had wonderful views, and whenever I visited her I'd think to myself, *Now, this is a gorgeous place—I sure wouldn't mind living here.* She and I were talking one day, and she told me she wanted to sell it. I got all excited, thinking, *Gee, maybe . . . maybe.* We had been wanting a bigger house and this one would give us the space without the inconvenience of having to build. I couldn't stop thinking about it, and when Phillip came home I told him that Leigh was putting her house on the market and I wanted him to see it.

IF PHILLIP AND I GET ALONG WELL, IT'S NOT BE-CAUSE WE AGREE ON EVERYTHING; IT'S BECAUSE WE BOTH MAKE AN EFFORT TO UNDERSTAND WHY THE OTHER IS THINKING, FEELING, OR ACTING A CERTAIN WAY.

So we went and looked at the house. Phillip really liked it and I really loved it. I was already picturing our furniture in the rooms and designing window treatments and imagining the meals I could cook in the gourmet kitchen. The one downside was that the asking price was more than we had spent on our current house, so we were going to have to decide whether or not the financial angle made sense.

When we got home I went on and on about how much I loved the house and how great it would be for the kids. Phillip listened patiently, then looked up and spoke. "You know what, Robin," he said, "I'm going to try to buy that house for us. But if I get into dealing for the house and they don't take what I offer, the deal is over, and I'm really concerned that I'm going to upset you and you're not going to be happy. But you need to know I will not risk more than we can afford for that house just to make you happy. I want you to be prepared for that. I want you to have the house. But I'm really afraid I'm going to upset you if I come back and say, 'We can't make a deal,' because I'm not going to risk any more than I know I can afford."

He was gazing at me intently with this worried look on his face, and I thought, *What a precious man. Here he is, doing his job to protect our livelihood and our family, and he's still concerned about disappointing me.* I walked around to where he was standing, wrapped my arms around his waist, and laid my head on his back.

"Where am I right now?" I said.

"You're right behind me," he said.

"That's right," I said. "And don't you ever forget it."

I felt him exhale and relax in my arms.

We ended up not buying the house on the hill. The deal wasn't right for us, and Phillip thought it best to let it go. And as much as I liked that house, it was easy for me to let it go because I knew that if Phillip didn't think it was right for our family, it wasn't meant to be, end of story. Nothing—no thing—could be more precious than my trust for my husband and my belief that he had, and has, our family's best interests at heart.

Believe me, I'm a girl who enjoys her stuff. I love having beautiful things, and wearing pretty clothes, and living in a gracious house in a lovely part of town. But these are only possessions; as long as my husband and I can have true joy in one little corner of our house, all the stuff surrounding it doesn't matter. It doesn't matter where we live: we once lived in a place that wasn't much bigger than my closet is now, and if we had to, I could move back to that apartment and be very fulfilled (a bit cramped, maybe, but fulfilled).

What matters to me is the way I felt Phillip relax when I told him I was right behind him. I felt a peace about him at that moment because he knew what I meant: Don't worry, Phillip. *Don't ever worry about disappointing me because I am right behind you. I trust you, and I know that you're going to make the right decision for our family. I'm on your side; I'll always be on your side.*

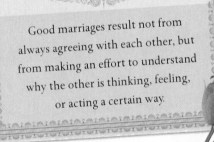

LIFE LESSON

Good marriages result not from
always agreeing with each other, but
from making an effort to understand
why the other is thinking, feeling,
or acting a certain way.

FRIENDSHIP

THERE ARE SOME WOMEN WHO TOUCH OUR
HEARTS AND MINDS AND, IN SO DOING,
NURTURE OUR SOULS.

WHAT FRIENDS ARE FOR

GIRLS JUST WANT (AND NEED) TO HAVE FUN

WILD, WONDERFUL WOMEN

DON'T GIVE AWAY YOUR POWER

WOMEN OF GRACE

THE LIFE YOU ARE MEANT TO LIVE

REMEMBER, WE ALL STUMBLE, EVERY ONE OF US.
THAT'S WHY IT'S A COMFORT TO GO HAND IN HAND.

— *Emily Kimbrough*

Are For

One day our publicist came in to brief us on stories about us that would soon be appearing in the press. We usually have an idea about the fantasy of the week, but we don't comment on the stories, and in fact we don't read them anymore. At first they were bothersome but it doesn't take long to get a pretty thick skin. So anyway, one day our publicist comes in and says, "Robin, a story is coming out next week that says you hate it out here and that you're bored and lonely because you miss your bunco league, and that you wish you could have a baby girl." This was a total fabrication, of course.

Sure enough, this preposterous story appeared in the paper, describing me as out of my element and in need of friends, wandering the streets of Beverly Hills, going door to door like a hungry dog and saying, "Hello, do you bunco? Do you bunco?" And the story actually said that women would come to their doors and look at me as if to say, "Oh, you silly little Texas girl! This is Beverly Hills—we don't play bunco here."

Whatever. When you live in the public eye, you have to learn to roll with the punches. And I learned to do that by following some good advice from my dear friend Oprah.

Something papers regularly do is print stories about how Dr. Phil is bitterly feuding with Oprah. Now, you will never meet a woman sweeter than Oprah Winfrey, and they have never had a cross word. She is so proud of us both. She is kind and abundantly generous in every sense of the word.

WHEN YOU LIVE IN THE PUBLIC EYE, YOU HAVE TO LEARN TO ROLL WITH THE PUNCHES. AND I LEARNED TO DO THAT BY FOLLOWING SOME GOOD ADVICE FROM MY DEAR FRIEND OPRAH.

It was Oprah, after all, who first invited Phillip to appear on national television, and it was her idea that Phillip should have his own show. And it is a measure of her character that, when Phillip was offered his own show and it became clear we would be moving out west, she reacted like a mother when her kids go off to college.

I remember her calling when we first got here, asking how I was doing. Next week, same deal. "How are you? Do you need anything?" Thankfully, she has nothing to worry about: I thrive on change, and Phillip and I love it out here. But that just shows how sweet Oprah is, and how upsetting it is when a story comes out pitting Phillip against this woman who is his partner, his champion, and one of my dearest friends.

I remember one of these feuding stories coming out not long after we got here, and I called Oprah up to tell her how bad we felt that people were being misled into thinking Phillip and she were fighting. And she said to me, "Robin, this is what they do. They sit around the table on Monday morning and they say, 'Okay, what can we write about this week? What's hot?'" And she explained that if there isn't some real gossip, they'll say, "There's nothing really happening right now . . . so, who's hot? Who can we write about?" And they'll start throwing out names and create their own stories.

How glad I was then—and still am—for the gift of Oprah's wisdom and friendship. I think God places the right people in our lives at just the right moment, and they have unique ways of helping us with whatever life is throwing our way.

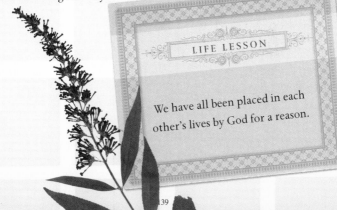

LIFE LESSON

We have all been placed in each other's lives by God for a reason.

WHOEVER IS HAPPY WILL MAKE OTHERS HAPPY TOO.
— *Anne Frank*

GIRLS JUST WANT (AND NEED)

to Have Fun

I'm in the audience at Phillip's show every single day, and sometimes Phillip will ask me something on-camera—there are certain times when he just needs a good dose of a woman's perspective. Other times, we'll tape an *Ask Dr. Phil and Robin* show, and I'll be up on stage with him to answer questions for our guests.

During one of these shows, a woman brought her friend on the show because she never took time for herself. She never got her hair done, all her clothes were hand-me-downs, and she basically never put herself first. She felt that all her time should go to her husband and kids.

Her story was one close to my heart, because I lost my mother at the age of fifty-eight because she never did anything for herself—she never went to the doctor, she never went to the beauty shop, she never even took the time to put her feet up. And so I told this woman, "You were a woman before you were a mother. You cannot allow yourself to forget the woman that you are just because you've become a mother. I think it is a simple decision to take care of yourself. Make it a choice of yours that you deserve to come first, that you deserve to have the kind of life you want to live as a woman, as well as your wife and mother roles."

WE NEED TO GO OUT WITH OUR GIRLFRIENDS EVERY NOW AND THEN. WE NEED THAT KIND OF SOCIAL ENERGY, AND WE JUST PLAIN NEED TO HAVE FUN.

I have never felt guilty about taking time for myself. It has always been a priority to give myself some time because I think as a wife and mother, I owe it to myself to do that, to take care of myself so I can be a better wife and mother. And as women, part of taking care of ourselves is allowing ourselves a little girl time. We need to go out with our girlfriends every now and then. We need that kind of social energy, and we just plain need to have fun.

I love going on weekend trips with friends; I love sitting around my sister's kitchen table playing cards and catching up on family news. I think it's important for every woman to know what she needs to be happy and fulfilled, and to do those things that will enrich her life. And I think if you ask your girlfriends, they'll tell you they need fun time just as much as you do. We all need times of kicking back and encouragement to reenergize us and replenish our emotional resources.

On the show that day, Phillip told that young mother, "If you're emotionally unavailable because you've worn yourself out, that's no gift. It's not necessarily selfish to take care of your children's mother." We have to take time for ourselves in order to best care for the ones we love.

LIFE LESSON

In order to take care of others, we have to take care of ourselves; and in order to take care of ourselves, we need to allow ourselves a little fun time.

THAT IS THE BEST—TO LAUGH WITH SOMEONE BECAUSE
YOU BOTH THINK THE SAME THINGS ARE FUNNY.

— *Gloria Vanderbilt*

WILD,

Wonderful Women

One way to take time for yourself, as well as get in some girl-friend time, is to attend a women's conference or retreat in your area—or travel to a different city and make a mini-vacation of it. There are a lot of wonderful conferences out there that aim to help you improve your life.

This year, I've had the privilege of being a featured guest speaker with an organization called Women of Faith. This group of incredible women holds conferences designed to help women connect with each other and grow mentally, emotionally, and spiritually. The Women of Faith speakers are loving, they're supportive, they're passionate. But first and foremost, they are hilarious.

The stories they share from the platform are so honest and funny; they share their experiences with kids, in-laws, and husbands completely openly, not pulling a single punch. But I think the main reason they connect with the audience so well is that they are real women who openly share their struggles. Patsy Clairmont, for example, is a former agoraphobic who was once too fearful even to get out of bed. And Marilyn Meberg came on the *Dr. Phil* show once—at the request of her friend and fellow Women of Faith speaker Luci Swindoll—seeking support for her germophobia.

My first conference was in Fort Lauderdale, Florida. I was a little nervous about speaking, and about sharing the stage with such accomplished speakers. This was the first time I have ever been in front of a big group or speaking in front of a crowd—and wouldn't you know, the crowd was 22,000 women! But when I got up there, the love, the support, the warmth of the audience just engulfed me. My talk went by a lot faster than I thought it would, and I actually walked off the stage excited about doing it again.

THIS IS WOMEN AT THEIR BEST: LAUGHING AND CRYING TOGETHER, OVERCOMING LIFE'S BIGGEST STRUGGLES, AND LIVING LIFE WITH PASSION.

And I think that's what's special about these conferences, the love and sisterhood that fill the stadium. When you see these women onstage, you notice how much they enjoy each other and how much fun they have together. Several of them have been friends for decades, and they all seem to share a bond: a love for life and a love for fun.

This is women at their best: laughing and crying together, overcoming life's biggest struggles, and living life with passion.

Attending a conference like Women of Faith might be just what you need to get out of your routine, have some fun girl time, and discover new ways to reach for the life you want.

LIFE LESSON

Loving friendship among women enables us to accomplish and overcome just about anything.

WE CAN'T CONTROL WHETHER WE WIN OR
LOSE, BUT WE CAN CONTROL OURSELVES.
— *Lisa Fernandez*

DON'T GIVE AWAY

Your Power

Phillip had this one relative I couldn't figure out. One day this person would act as if I were the best thing that had ever happened to the family, the next, as if I were an evil person who didn't deserve to live. At family gatherings I'd come in all cheery and friendly and everything would be fine until the two of us would end up alone in a room together and this person would make a critical remark and leave me standing there, stung and reeling with confusion.

I took it very personally. Why was this person treating me this way? I wasn't about to make a scene; this was Phillip's family and I was the newest part of it. It was my job to be sweet, and (the way I saw it) it was Phillip's job to manage his family and make them treat me properly. So I would tell Phillip about these episodes and wait for him to say, "Robin, you are the kindest, most loving person on the planet, and no one has the right to treat you this way. I'm going to go over and straighten things out once and for all."

But he never said that. What he consistently said was, "You know what? This person did have the right to say that." And man, every time he said it, it felt like he'd slapped me. I felt like saying, "Now, wait a minute, buddy—you're supposed to be on my side!"

THE MOMENT I ACCEPTED THIS PERSON'S RIGHT TO BE CONFLICTED AND IN TURMOIL, I WAS ABLE TO RESTORE MY OWN EQUANIMITY.

And he would look at me in his levelheaded way and say, "No, Robin. You're not going to convince me otherwise. This person had the right to say it. *But you have the right not to react to it.*" Whenever I went to Phillip for comfort, he'd say, "No, they had every right to say that," which drove me wild because I thought he was telling me that he agreed with this person. But the essence of what he was telling me, every time, was, *You can't control other people. People have the right to think and say whatever they want to. But you have the right not to take it to heart, and not to react.*

I didn't like hearing it, but Phillip kept repeating it until one day a light bulb went on in my head and I realized, *He is neither betraying me nor agreeing with his relative. The reason he has this calmness about him is because he is dismissing this person's comments as nonsense, and he thinks I should do the same.*

He was right. And from that day forward, I have taken to heart this important relationship principle: what other people think of me or say about me ought not to influence what I know to be true about myself. To doubt myself because of others would be to hand over my power to them, and that is something I will not do. I never give my power away.

That's exactly what you do when you allow someone else's opinion of you to affect your opinion of yourself: you're giving away your power. And I say, don't do it. This family member truly felt righteous about judging me harshly, but what I failed to see at the time was that the judgment was more about that person than it was about me. Some combination of irrational thoughts, distorted perceptions, and unknowable events in that person's life had motivated those behaviors. Ultimately (and ironically), it had nothing to do with me. The moment I accepted this person's right to be conflicted and in turmoil, I was able to restore my own equanimity. I now enjoy a warm relationship with this person because I made a decision to allow in only the positive aspects of the relationship and to reject the bad ones. I could not control this person, but I could control myself.

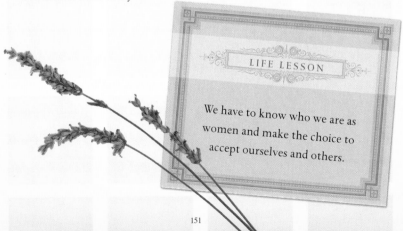

LIFE LESSON

We have to know who we are as women and make the choice to accept ourselves and others.

FLOWERS NEVER EMIT SO SWEET AND STRONG A FRAGRANCE
AS BEFORE A STORM. WHEN A STORM APPROACHES THEE,
BE AS FRAGRANT AS A SWEET-SMELLING FLOWER.

— *Jean Paul Richter*

WOMEN OF

Grace

Writing this book has made me even more aware of the women who have touched my heart and mind, and, in so doing, nurtured my soul.

One of them is my sister Cindi, whose courage and grace in the face of unspeakable suffering have inspired me with awe. Cindi and her boyfriend were driving to the airport early one morning when a maniac on an overpass dropped a jug of sulfuric acid through the windshield of her car, studding her with glass, catastrophically burning her face and body, and shattering her life. My poor, dear sister was horribly burned over vast portions of her face and body, and her recovery included ghastly episodes of debridement, when her burned, dead skin would be sloughed away from the raw, living tissue beneath it. Cindi would return from these sessions in utter agony, looking as if she had been flayed alive, and I'd wonder, *Why, Lord? Why Cindi? Why did this happen to this loving, gentle soul?*

Even today, more than five years later, it's hard for me to discuss the event without wanting to scream and shake with rage about the injustice of it all. But Cindi does not. My amazing sister chooses to see the experience not as a vicious attack against her but precisely for what it was: a random, barbaric act directed at no one in particular by a human being with a profound indifference to human suffering. Cindi knows there is nothing she could have done to avoid or prevent the catastrophe; it was out of her control. She believes that as much as she has suffered (and she has, horribly), there are people who suffer more than she, and for just as little reason. She never felt sorry for herself or expressed grief over her disfigurement. She never cursed the person who did this to her.

This will give you an idea of the pure goodness of my sister's soul. A few years after the attack, Cindi and I appeared on *Larry King Live*. Her memoir had just been published and Larry, an old friend of Phillip's and mine, suggested she and I come on the show.

Sitting opposite him at that little desk, I could tell from the look in his eyes that he was devastated for Cindi. Under the unforgiving glare of television studio lighting, he looked at Cindi's scarred face and asked, "Do you ever think, *Why me? God, why me?*"

Cindi sat quietly for a moment before speaking. "No, I've never thought that, not once," she said. "If I asked God, 'Why me?' it would mean that

I thought it should have happened to someone else. And I could never wish this on someone else."

What an amazing woman—what generosity, what love, what strength! Above all, what grace. Not once did she blame God or express anger that He had done this to her. She never believed that God meant for this terrible thing to happen, for that would have meant she believed she deserved to suffer. This is a prime article of faith both for her and for me: God is there to love us and give us strength. I was proud of her for not caving in to despair and for choosing forgiveness instead. In so doing, she reclaimed her life from horror and insisted on her God-given right to live out her time here on earth.

The choices Cindi has made since the accident, the attitude she has maintained, have in turn inspired me to make those kinds of choices. My sister has inspired me and countless others to become women of grace and resolve.

LIFE LESSON

The people in our lives often inspire us to become more generous, more loving, more graceful.

IT IS ONE OF THE GREATEST GIFTS FOR ME TO KNOW THAT I HAVE PURPOSE BEYOND MYSELF.

— *Pat McCormick*

THE LIFE

You Are Meant to Live

I said at the beginning of this book that I believe we were put on this earth to enjoy lives of joy and abundance. My wish is for you to perceive, as I do, the presence of God within us and around us and feel the love He feels for us all. I have total peace in my heart because I know I can turn to God at any time and ask for help. I know I can. That's why I get out of bed every morning and before I go to sleep every night, I thank God for all that He has blessed me with.

There will always be people who want to tell you who you should be and what you should do, but no one can tell you how to live your life because there is no one quite like you. Look inside yourself with open eyes and see who's really in there—not your mother or your father, not your husband or your children, but *you*. Go deep, really deep, beyond the labels of wife and mother, daughter and sister, until you find the essential woman inside, the woman God created. See her, embrace her, and honor her by insisting on your right to choose the life you are meant to live.

My hope is that you will see your life as I see mine, as a vast array of choices that can bring you closer to the person you long to be. My dream is for you to bring into your life whomever you cherish and whatever you desire by deciding, as I have, precisely who you are and what you need to be happy. Your life is waiting for you to claim it; it's all in the choosing. May you choose wisely and well.

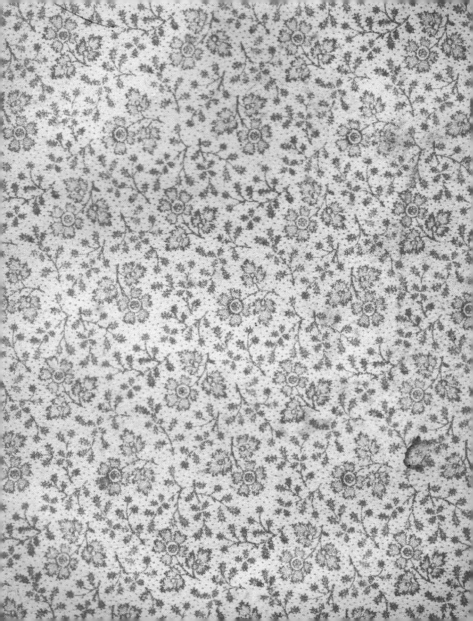